C0-BWW-312

**"I'm an obstetric surgeon. Caleb Stride."
He held out his hand.**

An obstetric surgeon? Now her mind saw him in scrubs, and that did wonders for her libido, too. Fighting it down, she smiled at him and shook his hand, thrilling at the electric shocks that ricocheted up her arm at the contact.

"Dr. Rory Dotson. I'm an obstetric surgeon, too, here at St Henry's. Where are you based?" she asked, hoping he'd confirm he was safely at a hospital far, far from her own, as she *never* indulged in workplace flings.

"I've been working in San Diego the last couple of years, but I'm looking for new opportunities to present themselves."

San Diego? Excellent. *So no chance of me running into you ever again after tonight and that makes you perfect.*

She licked her lips, drawing his eye, exactly as she'd expected, seeing the hunger in his expression. The need that she also felt.

Dear Reader,

I love writing about getting pregnant with twins. It happened to me, so it's special when I get to write about it, too. I remember the shock at the twelve-week ultrasound, reaching for my mother-in-law's hand and asking the sonographer, "Are you sure?" We both cried and I remember being gutted that my husband wasn't there for it. He'd gone to an emergency dental appointment and as this was my second pregnancy, he'd been to all the first pregnancy's scans and I'd said to him, "Don't worry about missing it, you've seen it all before."

So when I got to tell him it was twins, he thought I was playing a practical joke on him! And then I showed him the scan pics. Baby A and Baby B. Mine were non-identical, a girl and a boy, and my son and daughter make me so very proud every single day. I like to imagine that Rory and Caleb, the hero and heroine of this story, go into the future feeling that way, too.

I hope you enjoy their story.

Warmest wishes,

Louisa x

ONE NIGHT TO
TWIN MIRACLE

LOUISA HEATON

◆ Harlequin

MEDICAL ROMANCE

If you purchased this book without a cover you should be aware that this book is stolen property. It was reported as "unsold and destroyed" to the publisher, and neither the author nor the publisher has received any payment for this "stripped book."

H Harlequin®
MEDICAL
ROMANCE

Recycling programs
for this product may
not exist in your area.

ISBN-13: 978-1-335-99332-8

One Night to Twin Miracle

Copyright © 2025 by Louisa Heaton

All rights reserved. No part of this book may be used or reproduced in any manner whatsoever without written permission.

Without limiting the exclusive rights of any author, contributor or the publisher of this publication, any unauthorized use of this publication to train generative artificial intelligence (AI) technologies is expressly prohibited. Harlequin also exercises their rights under Article 4(3) of the Digital Single Market Directive 2019/790 and expressly reserves this publication from the text and data mining exception.

This is a work of fiction. Names, characters, places and incidents are either the product of the author's imagination or are used fictitiously. Any resemblance to actual persons, living or dead, businesses, companies, events or locales is entirely coincidental.

For questions and comments about the quality of this book, please contact us at CustomerService@Harlequin.com.

TM and ® are trademarks of Harlequin Enterprises ULC.

Harlequin Enterprises ULC
22 Adelaide St. West, 41st Floor
Toronto, Ontario M5H 4E3, Canada
www.Harlequin.com

HarperCollins Publishers
Macken House, 39/40 Mayor Street Upper,
Dublin 1, D01 C9W8, Ireland
www.HarperCollins.com

Printed in U.S.A.

Louisa Heaton lives on Hayling Island, Hampshire, with her husband, four children and a small zoo. She has worked in various roles in the health industry—most recently four years as a community first responder, answering emergency calls. When not writing, Louisa enjoys other creative pursuits, including reading, quilting and patchwork—usually instead of the things she *ought* to be doing!

Books by Louisa Heaton

Harlequin Medical Romance

Christmas North and South

A Mistletoe Marriage Reunion

Cotswold Docs

Best Friend to Husband?
Finding a Family Next Door

Night Shift in Barcelona

Their Marriage Worth Fighting For

Yorkshire Village Vets

Bound by Their Pregnancy Surprise

Single Mom's Alaskan Adventure
Finding Forever with the Firefighter
Resisting the Single Dad Surgeon
The Surgeon's Relationship Ruse

Visit the Author Profile page
at Harlequin.com for more titles.

To my twins, Becca and Jared x

Praise for
Louisa Heaton

"Another enjoyable medical romance from
Louisa Heaton with the drama coming courtesy of
life on a busy maternity ward. Lovely characters, a
great story, set in one of my favourite cities and an
all round easy engaging read."
—*Goodreads* on *Miracle Twins for the Midwife*

CHAPTER ONE

DR AURORA DOTSON wasn't used to having a thriving social life. Most of her hours were spent at London's St Henry's Hospital, in scrubs, hair tied up in a messy bun with a pen poked through it, grabbing a Belgian chocolate from the box on Reception whenever she had a moment and sharing a dirty joke and a laugh with the midwives.

So tonight she was out of her comfort zone, attending a charity auction to raise money for the NICU at the Augustine Hotel, and scrubs simply would not do. The Augustine was one of the oldest and finest hotels in London, five star, à la carte dining, marble floors and *suites*—all of which had names—rather than rooms. It demanded a dress, heels and make-up, of which she'd had none—unless an ancient mascara counted, which she was sure it did not.

Luckily, her sister, Maylee, had stepped in to rescue her, offering Aurora one of her dresses to wear and the use of her make-up bag for the big night.

'Honestly, Rory, what would you do without me?'

She'd chosen a simple, little black dress with an asymmetrical neckline that fell just above the knee. She'd teamed it with some dainty black heels that threatened to break her ankles from their vertiginous heights, and had sat patiently whilst Maylee had painted her face, because Rory had no idea in what order everything should be used.

When her sister was done, she had looked in the mirror and marvelled at her own reflection. 'How did you do that?'

The heels were taking some getting used to. One dangerous wobble near the hotel lifts had her considering taking them off, going barefoort and walking into the venue swinging them from her fingers, but she wasn't sure her bosses would be that impressed, so she'd simply reminded herself to walk really slowly. And it was a decision she was glad of because, when the doors opened and she stepped inside the room, she gasped at the marvel before her and needed some time to take it all in.

The Augustine had a beautiful function room, with hints of the old theatre it used to be. There was a stage for the VIPs, a pit for the orchestra that was playing…who on earth was paying for that? There was also a large space decorated with red curtains, candles, a massive candelabra dripping with crystals that hung from the ceiling, and gilt-framed pictures on the walls of all the past artistes who had performed here over the years.

A waiter appeared at her side holding a silver tray laden with champagne flutes. She took one and slowly began to make her way into the throng of people. As an obstetric surgeon at St Henry's, the NICU was an area dear to her heart, and it needed funding for the state-of-the-art incubators and other equipment that it wanted to buy. Her bosses had made it clear that she was to attend, schmooze the guests and make it clear how important their donations could be. She thought it best to find one of the board first, just to make sure that they could see that she had *at least* attended. She wasn't sure how persuasive she'd be in making people part with their money. All she had to do was find them.

Luckily one of them, Charles Holloway, had quite the distinctive braying laugh. Once she heard it, she set off in that direction, excusing her way through the crowds and making her way over to a large group of black suits, where Charles held court.

'And she was just stood there! Without a stitch!' Charles burst into a loud, donkey-like laugh, knowing that all the sycophants surrounding him would laugh too. She assumed he'd been telling one of his bawdy jokes, as he was prone to do when surrounded by gentlemen, but she made her way into his inner circle and raised her hand in greeting.

'Mr Holloway. Good evening.'

'Dotson! Hardly recognised you in your glad rags. Good to see you here.'

She felt his hungry gaze assess her and waited for it to be over. Later on she'd take a shower, but for now she would endure it. Charles, weirdly, was a friend of a friend who had known her father's family for years. He was a bit of a pig, but she'd been told he had put in a good word for her when she'd applied for her post at St Henry's. It had been made clear to her that she had him to thank, even though she felt very strongly that her application had been strong enough on its own, without his greasy input.

Charles introduced her to the gentlemen of his circle and she nodded and smiled at them all, shook a few hands, fulfilled her duty and was about to mention that she'd seen someone she needed to speak to when Charles took her to one side.

'There's someone I need you to schmooze.'

'Really?' She didn't want to schmooze anyone.

'Yes, see that fella over there?' He pointed at a stooped old man with a cane in a dark-grey suit, talking to a woman of similar age in a crimson dress. 'Billionaire. William Stride. Deals in diamonds, would you believe, but his grandson needed an incubator when he was born, which is why he is here tonight. Feels the need to give something back. I think you should go and talk to him.'

'Oh, I'm not sure if I—'

'Course you can! He's always been a sucker for a pretty face, otherwise I'd be talking to him.' Charles chortled at his own self-deprecating yet sexist joke as he nudged her forward.

Rory hated being used this way. But weren't they all here to charm people into opening their wallets and purses and pouring money the hospital's way? That was part of the job, whether she liked it or not. And what would it hurt to say hello and introduce herself—maybe tell the gentleman a few stories? He might be nice, sweet. And anyone at this point would be better than Charles. 'Fine.'

She made her way through the crowd, grabbing a second champagne flute after emptying the first, and surreptitiously made her way towards the old couple. As the crowd began to clear and she got closer, she could see that they were not standing talking to one another alone. There was someone else there—a guy her age. A guy with a charming, bright smile who seemed genuinely interested in something the older man was saying, laughing with them.

She couldn't help but notice how good he looked in his tux, the colour of it pairing beautifully with his dark hair and bright-blue eyes. Eyes that seemed to glance briefly in her direction and catch her gaze. In that millisecond of connection she felt a fizz of something explode within her and her heart began to pound, before he turned back to the older man and laughed again. She knew what that connection meant. She understood her attraction to this man…and why wouldn't she be attracted? He was gorgeous, whoever he was.

The unexpectedness of this other man already had her slowing and faltering. If William Stride had been alone, she simply would have gone up to him and said, *Mr Stride? Hello. I'm Dr Dotson. I'm an obstetric surgeon with this hospital; very pleased to meet you.* Then she'd have launched into her party patter, being polite, being political, selling the hospital and all the wonderful things they achieved there, in the hope of greasing the wheels a little bit.

But this other guy there, he'd see right through it. To be fair, so might William, but manners would simply prevent him from mentioning her obviousness out loud, because his need to be polite to a young lady would subdue anything else.

So, how to approach? Rory looked back and saw that Charles had already forgotten about her and moved on back to his cronies. Would he know, if she chose to avoid Mr Stride? *Probably not.* So she turned and headed in the other direction, hoping to find something to eat at the buffet table.

Smiling at last, she found a veritable array of delicious delights awaiting her: salmon bites; mini arancini; vegetable sushi; petits fours. And, strangely, tiny sausages on sticks with chunks of apple. Rory picked one up and tasted it, her mouth exploding with flavour.

'Changed your mind?' a voice said close to her ear.

Rory turned to see who it was, blushing madly when she realised it was the young man who had been talking to William Stride. The man who had caused her to divert because, well, he was quite the distraction.

Rory liked a good-looking man. A good-looking man was usually quite happy to join her for an hour or two of fun and then go his separate way. And, whilst she was happy for that to be her modus operandi, it had not been scheduled for tonight. Tonight wasn't for the hospital—not really. Tonight was for all those future babies who would be born and rely on the hospital's equipment and trained staff to look after them so that they got past their difficult start in life and grew up to live their best lives.

She smiled at him. 'About what?'

'Talking to my grandfather.'

'That was your grandfather?' Too late she realised she'd admitted that his grandfather had indeed been her target. But it also meant that she'd learned that this young man might just be the grandson who had needed a NICU incubator when he had been born, as Charles had informed her.

'Yes.' The man opposite her smiled and there was something about his smile that did strange things to her insides. This guy was utterly charming. Dangerously so, without even trying. His looks ought to come with a sign: *warning—irresistible.* His blue eyes sparkled, yes, but beyond that they seemed able to see deep into her soul, making her want to look away before he saw too much. His mouth was wide, generous and genuine. His eyes crinkled at the corners and his jawline was square and already prickling with the stubble that would be his five o'clock shadow. At the thought, her mind happily provided her with an image of his face resting on her lovely white bed pillows, those eyes gleaming at her with devilish wickedness at the memories of what they'd got up to the night before...

'I was going to say hello, sure, but then I saw you talking to him and I didn't want to interrupt.

I had no idea you were related.' She hoped he'd believe her.

Whether he did or not, he made no indication. 'So, why are you here this evening?'

Rory smiled and sipped her champagne, running her gaze up and down his body. The man knew how to wear a tux. 'To raise money for a good cause. You?'

'Same.'

She could tell he was admiring her dress. Or maybe what lay *beneath* the dress. The thrill of their instant connection was electrifying. 'I see. And what is it that you do for a living?' The grandfather was in diamonds. Maybe he was too. She could imagine him sweating beneath the hot sun, bare-chested, his hands and clothes covered in dirt as he prised a rare diamond from the rock and held it up to the light.

'I'm an obstetric surgeon. Caleb Stride.' He held out his hand.

An obstetric surgeon? Now her mind saw him in scrubs, and that did wonders for her libido, too. Fighting it down, she smiled at him and shook his hand, thrilling at the electric shocks that ricocheted up her arm at the contact. 'Rory Dotson. I'm an obstetric surgeon too, here at St Henry's. Where are you based?' she asked, hoping he'd confirm he was safely at a hospital far,

far from her own, as she *never* indulged in workplace flings.

'I've been working in San Diego the last couple of years, but I'm looking for new opportunities to present themselves.'

San Diego? Excellent. *So no chance of me running into you ever again after tonight and that makes you* perfect.

She licked her lips, drawing his eye and seeing the hunger in his expression, exactly as she'd expected. The need that she also felt. Rory didn't socialise often and when she did it was usually with a particular cause in mind: to connect with someone. It didn't have to end in sex, though if it did then that was a bonus. It was more about chasing the connection. About being someone's focus. About the flirting, the banter, the back and forth. That feeling of being special.

And if she decided to take it further? She chose her partners with care, making sure that they were someone who understood her one-night-only rule. There was no exchange of phone numbers. No exchange of email addresses or social media. It would be one night. That was it. Rory had no time, or inclination, to get into a complicated, difficult or disappointing relationship with anyone.

'And are you here alone tonight, Caleb?' She liked his name. It suited him. It was a strong name.

'I'm here with my grandfather.' He smiled, preferring to be a mystery man, clearly.

'That's not what I meant, and you know it. Are you in a relationship? Married?' He wore no ring, but that meant nothing these days.

'No.'

He looked directly into her eyes. His answer told her everything she needed to know. Charles's instruction to schmooze the fabulously rich diamond guy was forgotten, as was the idea that she'd mingle and feel as if she was still on the clock at work, even though she was at an evening function. Her nerves before coming here were forgotten, and the worry that she'd turn an ankle and end up on crutches. The intent in his eyes and, no doubt her own, was all that mattered. She knew that she did not want to stand here for much longer holding this empty champagne flute. She could think of something much more interesting to hold…

His expression told her, in no uncertain terms, that he felt the exact same way.

'Good. Well. I think I'm going to go to the ladies' room. Maybe I'll see you out there?'

She never used to be this forward with men; she'd always been passive. But, since her humiliation at the hands of her ex-fiancé, Leo, she'd made a vow that she would never let a guy make the decisions ever again. Which meant that she'd had to take control. Always. The first couple of times she had felt awkward, unsure if she could even be that kind of strong and assertive woman. But she figured if she could advocate for women at work, for her job, then she could advocate for herself too. And that meant leading the way herself, making it clear to any man she got involved with exactly what she wanted and expected from him. No more, no less.

Rory gave Caleb one last lingering and flirtatious look before she turned and walked away, knowing that he would watch her go, so adding a little sway to her hips. Not too much! She still wasn't sure with these heels. But enough to draw the eye and make him hunger for her.

She headed over to the ladies' room, her eyes scanning the hallway. There was another function room next to the one that they'd been in, and it looked empty. Good to know. In the bathroom, she checked her make-up, touched up her lipstick and added one more spray of perfume to her wrists as she gazed into the ornate mirrors above the sinks and adjusted her appearance. She made her hair just right and smoothed out the tight skirt, making sure it hugged her curves perfectly.

I'm ready.

She hoped beyond hope that, when she left the bathroom, Caleb would be waiting for her outside. She'd thought this evening would be boring, meant for networking, and she'd get home exhausted and ready to crawl into bed. But now this night looked a little more promising and she was here for it. It would be incredibly disappointing if he wasn't waiting for her as she hoped, after she'd made it clear to him what she wanted. Her need to feel a physical connection with him was almost overpowering. He was handsome, effortlessly sexy, and she had not been with a man for just over six months. It was time and he was perfect, because she'd never see him again after this evening. He worked in San Diego!

Inhaling a deep breath, she opened the door to the bathroom and smiled instantly at the sight of Caleb leaning casually against the doorjamb right outside. 'Hello.'

'Hello.' Okay—rule setting time. 'You should know that I don't make a habit of this and that anything that happens tonight between us is a one-off. One night only. No commitments. Do you agree?'

He didn't take any time to think about it. 'I agree.' Clearly he was a creature much like herself.

She had laid down her invite and he had accepted. There was nothing more to be said. She reached for his hand, felt her fingers tingle at the touch and drew him towards the empty function room, closing and locking the door behind them. It was darker in here, the sound muffled by the heavy red curtains.

She turned to face him. Her eyes searched his in the shadows of the room. The tension between them was taut, like a bow-string. She hadn't even touched him yet and already her body was thrumming with need, her every nerve-ending alight with sweet anticipation.

Rory reached for the bow-tie at his neck and pulled it loose.

He reached for her but, no, she took hold of his forearms and pushed them down. She would control this and she would only let him touch her when she was ready. She'd make him wait. Make him hold back, so that when she did release him he would be an animal—just the way she liked them to be at the end, their wildness controlled by her so that, even if they felt strong, they would in fact be powerless.

She slowly undid the buttons on his shirt, opening it up to reveal his strong, masculine chest, and pulling the shirt from his waistband. She slid his tux jacket off him, letting it drop to the floor. Then she opened his shirt, slowly revealing his powerful chest and his neat, flat stomach. He was a joy to behold. A feast for her eyes. A carved statue of manliness who looked as good as he smelt.

Again, he reached up to touch her and she stilled his hands. 'Not yet,' she whispered, smiling. Reassuring him that his time would come.

She stepped back, letting him see. Her fingers reached for the hem of her dress, pulling it upward to reveal her underwear. She'd put on a matching black lace number. Maylee might have cocktail dresses and heels ready to go, but Rory had always bought herself nice underwear, having read somewhere once that if a person felt good underneath their clothes, that confidence could carry them forward.

She knew she looked good. She'd never been a woman to flaunt her body, or womanly curves, but she knew she had them. Men appreciated her ample breasts, the curve at her waist and the bloom of her hips. She wasn't skinny, but average. The dark, lacy knickers drew his gaze exactly to where she wanted it. Her shapely thighs made her legs look longer than they were.

'Let me touch you?' he asked softly.

'Not yet,' she said, feeling the full, delightful force of her control over him and stepping back towards him, reaching for his belt and sliding it free to drop to the floor like a leathery snake. His erection stood proud in his trousers. She reached for it and watched with satisfaction as his eyes closed in bliss as her hand stroked him through the material. It felt large, hefty. Enough that she could imagine it inside her, and the thought thrilled her.

But the knowledge that they weren't in the privacy of a hotel room, with the luxury of time, forced her to move quicker than she usually would. This was a moment in time that she did not want to have disturbed. Now that she'd set her sights on him and decided upon him, she wanted to consume him, as much as she wanted him to consume her. Anyone could try the door at any moment. Anyone could fetch a key to unlock it. The illicit thrill added to her arousal.

'Do you want me?' she whispered, her lips against his skin before she let her tongue lick around his neck.

'I do,' he breathed.

'Do you have protection?'

'In my wallet.'

'Is it in your jacket?'

He nodded.

She let him retrieve it and took it from him, finally undoing the zip over his large erection and allowing his trousers to fall to the floor. He wore boxer shorts and he was just as impressive below the waist as he was above it. She wanted him inside her. As soon as possible.

Rory gazed into his eyes as she reached inside his boxers to stroke him some more, feeling the warmth and weight of him in her hand before she lowered them and revealed him. His need for her was clear and she dropped to her knees to tease him with her tongue and lick him for a moment, hearing him groan and moan before she slid the condom onto the length of him. Then she pulled him down to lie back upon the carpet and told him to take her, finally releasing him from his constraints.

He was over her in an instant, a predatory alpha-wolf standing guard over the meal that was his, before he lowered the weight of himself onto her. He kissed her, softly at first and then passionately, his lips, his tongue, tasting her mouth and her neck, hungrily feeling for her taut nipples through her dress. He trailed his mouth down over her stomach, lower and lower.

Rory arched her back at the contact, closing her eyes, losing herself in the bliss of surrender. As much as she loved to be in charge of these moments, there was something deliriously wonderful about submitting to them too. Of allowing the guy to do with her what he willed. But it was only because she felt safe with him that she allowed it, telling herself that she was still in control of this…somehow.

And then he was inside her, filling her, stretching her, making her gasp as he rode her, and rode her hard. Her shoulders and backside rubbed against the carpet, and she knew she would have carpet burns, but she didn't care. Every mark, every sore spot, would simply cause her to smile secretly to herself at the memories she would feed on for the next few months, until she felt the need for a connection once again.

As their movements became more frantic, as she felt her arousal building to its climax, she pushed herself up against him so that his body rubbed her just so, until her excitement exploded into a multitude of stars. Urged on by her orgasm, he came moments later, gasping and groaning, until he slowed then stilled, kissing her, breathing heavily and finally, sadly, withdrawing.

As always in these moments, Rory felt a thrill—power that she could make him do this, feel this. He was good. Exactly what she'd needed. Making him hold back in those early stages meant that, when she'd released him, when she'd let him touch her, it had been all about her. His need to hungrily explore, to touch, to taste, to caress, had made *her* the focus. Had made her feel as if she was precious. As if she was the one who'd got more: more attention, more soft touches. It had allowed her to revel in the feeling of being special. That was what this had all been about for her.

He'd been amazing, actually, and she found herself wondering what their encounter might have been like if they had had the security and privacy of a hotel room. Would it have lasted longer? Most definitely. But it hadn't. Adjusting her underwear, she stood and began to get dressed, smoothing her hair and her skirt. She slipped back into her heels as she watched him stand and remove the condom, not sure where to put it.

She had a tissue in her clutch and she wrapped it up in that and slid it into her bag. She would go to the bathroom and dispose of it in a moment. 'I think we should leave this room separately.'

'Agreed,' he said, breathless still, buttoning his trousers once again.

'I don't think we should show that we know each other in the function room.'

'As you wish.'

Rory smiled. Good; he was playing along, letting her control every aspect of this, which was how she liked things. This encounter had been unexpected and delightful, but now they both had to return to being the professionals they were. She would go back into the charity event and do her duty, knowing all the while their little shared secret was theirs alone. And after tonight? She would never have to see him again.

He would go back to San Diego. Leaving her with only a smile upon her face and a sticky sensation between her legs.

CHAPTER TWO

CALEB HAD BEEN born in St Henry's Hospital, so it felt strange to stand there and look at it and realise that his entire, crazy life had begun in this very place. And here he was, returning to work in the very department where his life had been saved.

His mother had come to this hospital in early labour at twenty-nine weeks' gestation. She'd been unwell, suffering from a urine infection that had spread to her kidneys, triggering contractions. The doctors had done what they could to try and prevent the early labour, but nothing had worked: Caleb had been born, struggling to breathe, and was placed into the NICU, plugged into machines to keep his tiny body alive and breathing. He'd had complications. He had developed an infection and had a small brain bleed, which often happened with preemies.

The doctors had gravely informed his mother that he might not pull through, as so much was assaulting his tiny body, but somehow he had. He'd defied expectations, and hearing that story as a small child had made him feel that he would spend his entire life defying expectations wherever he went.

At school, he'd excelled in every subject. He'd got the lead in the school plays every single time. He'd always been the captain of his school sports teams. He'd always been surrounded by girls who flirted with him and wanted to go out with him. And he'd been noticed and admired by everyone, except for the one person whose admiration he'd sought the most: his father.

But he refused to think of that man today. His father wasn't even in his life any more, except as a contact on his phone, and their message history was incredibly short and sporadic, with months between them. His father had made himself a new family, after he'd failed with his first one, and by all accounts he was failing the second one in the exact same way. Caleb wanted nothing to do with him.

Entering Reception, his gaze scanned the multitude of signs, looking for the maternity and delivery ward: floor B. Eschewing the lifts, he jogged up the stairs to the second floor, following the signs that led him to the ward. There was a woman by the doors, holding onto the wall as she breathed through a contraction, her birth partner behind her rubbing her back and coaching her through.

He passed on by and pressed the button to speak to Reception.

'Maternity, can I help?'

'Caleb Stride, obstetric surgeon.'

The door buzzed open and he walked through, eyes scanning the place, instantly noting the layout, how busy they were and how many staff seemed to be working. He was going to be covering for a surgeon who'd had her own baby, and he was kind of excited about the placement, wondering if the obstetrician he'd met at that charity event six weeks ago would be here.

It would be fun to see her face when he appeared. He'd walked away from that night feeling that she was a woman who liked to control things, and him turning up would be the last thing she'd expect. And he thought it would be fun to surprise her and put her on the back foot. He could be in charge for a change!

She'd told him that she had a one-night rule, which had been just fine by him, because he didn't get into serious relationships either. He'd borne witness to the pain and suffering his mother had gone through when his father had never been around and, though he strived not to be anything like his father, he was not going to risk further pain to someone else with his own demanding job.

He didn't do commitment, so that was some-

thing he and Rory had in common. It would be
fun to flirt with her and play with the line she'd
drawn in the sand. He wanted to show her that
her line was just that—in sand. It was something
that could be moved, smudged.

'Mr Stride?' The midwife on Reception had
red, curly hair and beamed at him.

'Hi, yes. I'm here covering for Ms Bakshi?'

'Oh, of course!' Was she blushing? He knew
the effect he sometimes had on women and it
always amused him. 'Right, okay. Well, I'm
Maddie. The rest of the team are on the ward,
otherwise I'd introduce you, but handover is in
fifteen minutes. Here, take this.' She passed him a
sticky note upon which she'd scrawled a four-digit
number. 'It's for the office, which is just down
there, end of the corridor on the right. Doctors
do their handover in there.' She smiled again, her
hand going to her hair subconsciously.

'Perfect, thanks. Oh, by the way, is Rory on
duty today?'

'Ms Dotson? Yes. You know her?'

His mind flashed with images from that dark
function room: the black triangle of lace against
the smooth expanse of her skin; the way her back
arched as she thrust upwards to meet him and
grind against him; the softness of her; the shadow
cast in the dip beneath her belly button. How

she'd tasted. How it had felt to bury himself in her. 'A little.' He smiled.

He headed down to the staff room, punched in the number on the door and pushed it open. He found a locker to deposit his jacket and backpack in. Then he turned and surveyed the room proper. It was pretty standard: a desk with a work station, plain walls, a changing room off to the right. There was a couch against the wall with cushions that had seen better days, and a square of tables, lined with chairs for maybe ten to fifteen people, with the remains of crumbs in the middle.

He stood and waited for the door to open.

Normally, she'd take the stairs to Maternity. But not today. She was either exhausted from working double shifts the last couple of days, or she was coming down with something, but Rory wasn't feeling her best. She was tired, mostly, with a weird headache just above her eyebrows. As she sometimes suffered with her sinuses, she hoped she wasn't about to get sinusitis. And, when she'd awoken this morning, her usual cup of coffee hadn't hit the spot at all. Maybe the milk was going off or something, but it just hadn't tasted right.

So she hit the button for the lift and tried to get her mind ready to face another busy day. She was on day shift today: eight until five-thirty. And, though she was exhausted already, she hoped for a busy day so that the time would go quickly. Rashid had informed her last week that they had secured a cover surgeon for Eesha Bakshi, so that was good, and apparently they started today. She would appreciate their skilled hands to help carry the load, as she'd been doing a lot of overtime lately.

The lift pinged open and she stepped inside. Just as the doors were closing, a woman slipped into the lift, overwhelming the small space with her overpowering perfume. Rory wrinkled her nose and turned away to breathe. The scent was sickly and nauseating. *Did she bathe in it? Jeez.* She tried to hold her breath, but it was almost impossible, so when the lift doors reopened on floor B Rory was quick to escape and breathe again. *Why did some people do that?*

As she headed down to Maternity, she spotted Lucy labouring by the door, her partner, Derek, rubbing her back. 'How's it going, Luce?'

Lucy Denby had come in late last night with contractions, just as Rory had gone off shift. She'd only been four centimetres dilated when Rory had left.

'Her contractions stopped for a few hours,' Derek said. 'But they've just started up again. She's at six centimetres.'

'Not long to go, eh? Keep active as much as

you can and you'll have a baby in your arms in no time.'

'Let's hope,' Lucy managed.

Rory swiped her card to let her onto Maternity and headed down the corridor towards Reception. Maddie, one of the midwives, was sipping from a cup. 'Do my eyes deceive me?' Rory asked in mock-shock. 'Is there *actual steam* coming from that cup?'

'Yep. Alert the media: midwife consumes a drink that's still hot.'

Rory laughed.

'New guy's here. I gave him the number to the handover room.'

'Oh. Brilliant.'

'You might want to tweak your look.'

Rory paused, confused. 'Huh?'

'He's bloody gorgeous! Looks like someone asked AI to come up with an image of a hot doctor. What with you being single, I thought you might want to do something about…that.' Maddie waved her pen in the general direction of Rory's hair. 'And that.' Next she waved her pen at Rory's face.

'What do you mean?'

'You're looking rough, girl, and I'm being polite.'

'Are you, though?' She smiled and stopped at the desk to get out a compact from her bag to check her appearance. Not that she was expecting to flirt with the new guy; she didn't do work flings, but hey, a girl had to have standards. She did look a little grey and her hair was messy from the wind outside. If this was what too many double shifts did to her, then maybe she ought to slow down.

But Rory adored her job. It gave her life. It was her reason for being and she didn't mind volunteering for extra shifts. St Henry's was her home, just as much as her tiny flat was. But here she got to see happy families, the miracle of birth and cute, chubby babies; and this was a happy place, mostly. 'Ugh. How do I fix this?'

'I think Plastics is on the next floor.' Maddie chuckled.

'You get sassy when you've had a hot drink!'

'Not sassy. Just want you to make a good impression on your friend.'

'My friend?'

'He says he knows you.'

'Knows me?'

'Yeah, um, Stride—Caleb Stride?'

Rory didn't recognise the name at first, her brain searching for the connection. When she did realise who it was Maddie was talking about, she felt her stomach drop and a blush flood her cheeks. She thought of him…*unbuttoning his shirt…caressing the bulge of his briefs. His gasps, his moans... Him thrusting himself into her... The carpet burn... Pleasure and pain...* 'He's meant to be in San Diego...'

'Oh, was that the accent? It was cute. How do you know him?'

She hoped the flush in her cheeks did not give away the answer.

It was many years since Rory had hidden in a toilet to avoid somebody, and she'd never thought that she would do so as an adult, but here she was. The last time, she'd been fifteen years old and hiding because a boy at the school dance had been horrified when she'd made a move to kiss him. Suspecting that all her classmates had witnessed it, she had raced to the nearest loo in sheer embarrassment to work out the easiest way she could collect her coat and escape without anyone noticing.

Now she stood staring at her pale reflection in the mirror, trying to work out exactly how she could fix the mess it reflected before she had to face Caleb once again. Standards mattered! He'd last seen her wearing her sister's finest, in make-up perfection, with her hair styled and her shapely figure on display at its best. Today, she wore a tee-shirt and jeans with an over-sized cardigan on top, because when she got to work she normally just changed into scrubs. It was easier—

there were usually a lot of fluids splashing about on Maternity. She'd twisted her dark hair up into a clip, her face was devoid of make-up and she had none with her, except for a year-old lip balm in the bottom of her bag.

Not that she was planning on flirting with the guy, or continuing anything that they had begun, no matter how fabulous their previous encounter. So, realistically, she ought to walk into that staff room looking a state and say, *Screw it. Take me as you find me, mister!* But she felt compelled to make herself look good for a guy that she'd slept with.

Rory began to feel sick at having to meet him again. She'd always been so careful to select sexual partners whom she would have no chance of meeting again, and she'd truly thought she was safe, because he'd said he worked in San Diego!

Damn.

She splashed water on her face, but that didn't help much. She pinched her cheeks to try to bring some colour into them, but she did look quite washed out, and hoped that it was just the bad lighting in the bathroom. She let her hair down from its clip and played with it this way then that, trying to make it look good, only to twist it back up into the clip again. She checked her watch. She couldn't be much longer. Handover would begin soon.

'I'm just going to have to face it out, aren't I?' she said out loud to the empty bathroom. 'Balls.' She did an about turn, and strode out of the bathroom and down the corridor towards the doctors' lounge, the butterflies in her nauseated stomach dancing gaily with delight at the unexpected situation. She paused briefly outside the door, then tapped in the keycode and swung it open.

And there he sat. On the couch, smiling up at her. 'Ms Dotson!'

She gave him a curt smile and nod, trying to show that his appearance didn't bother her in the least. 'Mr Stride.'

But he did bother her. He bothered her greatly. Because he looked just as delicious as he had at their first meeting, if not better, and now he was here and she didn't know how to deal with him. She headed straight to her locker, her armpits sweating, bundled away her bag and grabbed a fresh set of scrubs from storage, before squirrelling herself away into the changing room.

I'm just going to have to get through this.

The handover went as smoothly as they ever did, no matter where it was. The previous shift explained which patients they'd dealt with, if there'd been any developments or complications, who was on the list for surgery during day shift, who was assigned which cases to see on the ward and what jobs needed completing. Caleb sat taking notes throughout it all, sneaking peeks at Rory, who had managed to sit at the table further up from him so that she didn't have to look at him as Dr Marshall gave the handover from night shift.

She looked good—pale, but still beautiful, despite the fact that here she wore no make-up or figure-hugging clothes. She had a natural beauty that he adored to see. If he had to choose between natural beauty or a heavily made-up face, he'd choose natural every time. She'd been stunning the night of the charity event at the Augustine Hotel, even so. And the way she'd twisted her hair up into that clip… He could imagine letting it loose, watching it fall around her naked shoulders and running his hands through it. Smelling it. Nuzzling the nape of her neck and breathing her in.

Not that she'd let him. She'd made it clear that night that she had a one-night rule, and that was fine by him, but flirting would be fun anyway! Surely she'd enjoy that? And, if not, then she would tell him and of course he would stop.

'And I'd like to take this moment to welcome our new obstetric surgeon, Mr Caleb Stride, to the St Henry's family!'

Everyone turned to look at him, smile, nod or say hi. Even Rory turned, he noted, though she didn't smile or nod. She looked guilty. She looked a little sick. Had his presence here disturbed her that much?

'Mr Stride joins us to cover for Ms Bakshi and will be with us until Eesha decides when, or even if, she wants to return after having baby Zahir. Caleb, do you want to quickly just tell everyone a little bit about yourself?'

He nodded, confident. 'Hi guys, nice to meet you all. I'm looking forward to getting to know you all a lot better.' He looked at Rory as he said this, but she was looking down at the table and didn't notice. 'I've spent the last few years working over in the American healthcare system, but I'm back in Britain now and looking for a place to settle down near family, so here I am.'

Dr Marshall smiled. 'Good. Okay. I thought that Caleb could shadow you for today, Rory, is that okay?'

Caleb smiled at Dr Marshall's suggestion, his gaze drifting to Rory to see how she'd react. He saw her head lift quickly from her lap and her eyes widen briefly before she recovered and nodded. 'Yeah, sure.'

'Show him where everything is, get him accustomed as to how we do things. It might be worth him shadowing for this first week, actually, until he feels ready to settle in and do this UK style.' Dr Marshall chuckled.

'No problem,' Caleb said, finally making eye contact with Rory.

She looked…uncertain. Not the confident, take-charge woman that he'd met previously. Clearly his being here had put her on the back foot and she wasn't happy about meeting up with her one-night stand. He found it terribly amusing.

'Be gentle with me, Ms Dotson,' he said.

Her cheeks flushed with colour as everyone in the room laughed good-naturedly.

CHAPTER THREE

'WHY THE *HELL* aren't you in San Diego?' she asked, turning on him the moment they were alone. He was ruining everything, turning up like this, and she didn't like it one bit. Mostly because it broke her rule, but also because she was mad at herself. Mad for feeling her body react to his presence.

'Because I'm here,' he answered, smiling, a little bit amused by her consternation.

'You know this isn't ideal.' Rory risked a quick glance at Caleb as they headed to the ward to speak to their first patient. 'I don't fraternise with people I work with. It makes life complicated and I don't do complicated.'

'Are we fraternising right now?'

'No.'

'So we're okay, then. What happened was the past, Ms Dotson; you can relax. I'm not going to try and chase you up the aisle, you know.'

'Glad to hear it. This is where I work and I

won't have my reputation tarnished by any more gossip.'

Any more? Hmm. 'Understood. So, just flirt with you on the quiet, then?' He chuckled and she stopped to stare at him.

'No flirting! At all!'

He gave her a mock-salute and, flustered, she stomped past him, heading to Room One, sucking in a calming breath and relaxing her shoulders before she gently knocked on the door and pushed it open. 'Mrs Sanderson?'

'Yes?'

Mrs Sanderson had come in overnight on Dr Marshall's shift. Her water had broken at home and she'd been contracting steadily, but a nurse had noticed a rapid upturn in her temperature and suspected a possible infection.

'Hi. My name is Ms Dotson and this is Mr Stride. We're here to check you out and make sure you and baby are okay, seeing as you're not feeling very well. The nurse told you that you're running a fever?'

'Yes. I've been getting some chills too.'

'Okay.' Rory checked the file and noticed that Mrs Sanderson's waters had broken roughly eighteen hours ago. 'Any pain?'

'Yes, down here, but I thought maybe that was because of the contractions, though.'

'It could be.' She smiled, to try and show that

she wasn't too concerned yet, though there was a risk of a serious infection here. Some women could develop infections after the amniotic fluids had broken. 'Do you mind if I examine you?'

'Not at all.'

Rory performed a physical examination of the patient. She checked her blood pressure, which was still within the normal ranges, but she had evidence of tachycardia—a fast heart rate.

Caleb, she noticed, was checking the trace. Mrs Sanderson was strapped to the cardiotocography machine. The machine, also known as the CTG, not only monitored the baby's heart rate but also the length, strength and regularity of the mother's contractions. It was a vital piece of equipment in the labour room and could indicate early levels of distress to the baby that a midwife or doctor could otherwise not know about. It didn't hurt anyone, and the monitoring was conducted externally via the mother wearing two elasticated belts around her abdomen. Sometimes, if the baby's heart rate couldn't actively be monitored through the CTG, then internal monitoring would be used, wherein a clip would be attached to the baby's scalp.

'Baby's heart rate has increased. Has he or she been as active as they normally are?' he asked the patient.

'Not as much, no. Is that bad? I thought they all reduced movements during labour.'

'It's just something we need to be aware of, but they're not having decels, which is good.' Consistent decelerations could show that the baby wasn't happy.

Rory was worried about chorioamnionitis, an infection of the placenta and remaining amniotic fluid. 'Do you think you could do a urine sample for me? We can perform a rapid test of that, and I'd like to perform a more intimate exam with your permission to get a vaginal swab and check to see the colouration of your fluids.'

'Whatever you need to do.'

'Okay. I need to check your temp again. It was just over thirty-eight degrees an hour ago.'

Rory used the thermometer and discovered that Mrs Sanderson was still feverish. They unhooked the patient from the CTG machine and waited for her to use the bathroom. She waddled back into the room and passed them the sample. The rapid urine test indicated that there was a high white-cell count and, when Rory got the vaginal swab and performed the physical examination of Mrs Sanderson, she could smell the infection. It made her very concerned indeed.

'Okay. I'm just going to check to see if the bloods you had taken overnight have come back and then we'll formulate a plan, okay?'

'Is my baby going to be okay?'

'We're going to try and make sure of it.' Rory

glanced at Caleb to indicate that they should leave, and they headed back out into the corridor.

'You suspect chorioamnionitis?'

'Yes. The maternal fever, the tachycardia, the presence of purulence when I did the vaginal swab… Let's see what the bloods say, but I think we need to get antibiotics on board and this baby delivered asap, rather than wait, if we want to keep them both healthy.' Purulence was evidence of pus.

'Agreed. Want me to order those?'

'Please. Let's get her on ampicillin and gentamicin.'

'Will do.'

She watched him go, glad to feel her breathing return to normal as he walked away to use a terminal at the nurse's station. She opened up her tablet and tapped in her patient's details to bring up the blood results. Mrs Sanderson's CRP, her c-reactive protein, was raised considerably, indicating inflammation. She was also showing signs of leukocytosis, meaning her white blood cells that fought infection were also considerably raised. It was definitely looking like chorioamnionitis.

Returning to the room, they informed the patient of their findings and started her on the antibiotics. 'We're also going to start you on oxytocin to try and increase your contractions. The quicker baby is here, the better. If you consent to that, then we'll need to keep you on the CTG machine to monitor baby and make sure they're tolerating it, which also means you won't be able to move around as much.'

Mrs Sanderson nodded.

'Okay. We'll get your midwife, Sasha, to get that started in the next half hour, hopefully, and we'll keep you monitored and get you cracking on.' Rory smiled reassuringly.

'Thank you.'

'We've got you, okay?' she said, laying her hand on Mrs Sanderson's in a reassuring manner.

Her patient smiled, but her eyes were welling up as she fought to hold back tears.

Outside the room, Rory looked at Caleb. 'Why are you looking at me like that?'

He smiled. 'Like what?'

'Like you're thinking back to our last encounter.'

'I wasn't, but I am now.'

She shook her head in disbelief. 'I'm not sure this is going to work for me. I'm going to ask for you to be reassigned to another doctor to shadow for this week. I can't work with you looking at me like that.'

He held up his hands in mock-surrender. 'I'll stop.'

'You will?' She wasn't sure if she believed him, and a small part of her liked the fact that she'd had such an impact on him that he still thought about their encounter. *She'd* thought about it upon seeing him, so it was only fair…but having him think about it *in front of her* was weird. Because she wasn't used to seeing her very few sexual partners afterwards. And most certainly not at work!

Caleb got her flustered. She felt hot and sweaty and still a little bit sick. Her stomach was churning constantly, putting a weird taste in her mouth. 'I need to get a drink.'

Caleb stared into the NICU as he sipped his coffee on his morning break. Currently four incubators were occupied in the very room where he himself had been taken after his own birth. He wondered whereabouts, exactly. Over in the west corner that had hot-air balloons painted onto the walls? Or the east, where there were trees, bluebirds and a bright-yellow sun? He very much doubted it had been painted like that when he'd been a poorly baby. But, as he stood there and observed the parents sitting by the bedsides of their babies, he wondered how many hours his own mother had sat there and for how long she'd been by herself.

'Oh, God! You're here, too? I can't catch a break!'

He turned to see Rory coming through the security doors to the viewing window that allowed relatives to see into the NICU.

'Oh, I'm sorry. I thought the hospital was public property, but if I'm trespassing…?'

He smiled. There was something sweet about the way he disturbed her—as if their night had had much more of an impact on her than she was letting on, perhaps? Maybe she wanted more from him, but didn't want to admit that to herself, so she acted as though she didn't like him.

It reminded him of when he'd been at junior school and he'd been made by the teacher to sit next to Clare Maxwell. Clare had been really annoyed that he'd been placed beside her, physically drew a line down the centre of the desk and got upset whenever he accidentally strayed over it with an elbow or his pen. It had gone on for weeks, until one day she'd kissed him out of nowhere and they'd been boyfriend and girlfriend for a little while. It had been cute—sweet, innocent.

'It's just, this is my space. Where I come to chill. You're ruining it.'

'My apologies. I just wanted to see the space where I spent so much time as a baby myself.'

She paused from looking annoyed to look intrigued. 'Oh.'

'I was born at twenty-nine weeks. I stayed in here— he gestured at the space beyond with his coffee cup '—for nearly two months. My mother never missed a day.'

Rory came to stand by him. Not too close, he noted.

'And your father?'

Wow. She'd zeroed in on the one aspect that had always bothered him. She was astute. Maybe it had been in his tone when he'd only mentioned his mother. 'He came the first day, apparently, but he was a very busy man.'

Rory frowned. 'It can be hard for a parent to see their child looking so helpless.'

Caleb shook his head. That wasn't how it had been at all! 'I'd rather not talk about him, if you don't mind. Let's talk about us. That appears to be an easier subject,' he said, knowing that to her it was not. She tutted and turned away, glancing through the viewing window.

'So, you come here often?' he joked.

'As a matter of fact, I do. This room, this place, puts the rest of the world into perspective. If something bad happens, I come here and look into this room—at the babies, at the faces of the hopeful parents—and I'm reminded that, whatever I'm going through, it's never as scary as what's happening in here.'

'It makes you less frightened.' He understood implicitly because he did the same thing too.

'Yes.'

'So what brought you here today? Was meeting me again so terrible?' He said it like a joke, but he really hoped her answer wasn't yes. He'd enjoyed meeting up with her again, seeing her reaction, and he was glad to be here. He'd like to think that, somehow, a small part of her was glad to see him.

She smiled at him. 'You're not that important, Caleb. Sorry to disappoint you.'

'I'm hurt.' He grabbed a pen from his pocket and used it to act as if she'd just stabbed him in the heart.

'I had a headache. That's all. I didn't sleep well, and I just needed to come here and look at these families and be reminded of what the struggle is all about.'

'I get that.'

She looked up at him then, assessing him. 'Is what you said earlier the only reason you're here—at the hospital, in general?'

'I have many reasons for returning to London. Family is one of them.'

'Your grandfather... I met him at the charity ball...is he alright?'

Caleb nodded. 'He's fine. In Cape Town at the moment.'

'Good. He seemed a nice guy.'

'He's the best.'

So much better than his own father. But that wasn't a difficult achievement.

CHAPTER FOUR

THIRTY MINUTES BEFORE the end of their shift, they were called in to Mrs Sanderson's room, as she'd begun to push. They'd monitored her closely all afternoon and the monitoring had ramped up after the baby had opened its bowels and passed meconium whilst still inside the womb, indicating that maybe it wasn't as happy as it ought to be.

Rory and Caleb were called in for the delivery, along with the paediatric team and Special Care Baby Unit team, just in case there were any issues with its breathing when baby was born.

They gloved, gowned and got ready, Caleb positioning himself between Mrs Sanderson's stirrupped legs, whilst Rory checked on the CTG tracing.

'Another push, that's it. Deep breath, hold and push—one, two, three…' Caleb counted.

Mrs Sanderson was crowning. The dark smears of meconium could be seen on the baby's scalp. The real worry was whether the baby had inhaled any of it. Sometimes they didn't, but if they had, there'd be signs to look for: yellowish staining of the skin and nails, rapid breathing with abnormal breath sounds, an enlarged chest and signs that the rib muscles were working extra-hard to inhale and exhale.

'Nearly there, that's it...and push! Head's nearly out!'

She watched as Caleb checked for any cord around the baby's neck, but there didn't appear to be, and with one final push, and a gush of stained fluids, Mrs Sanderson's baby boy slithered free and screwed up his face in an attempt to cry.

Caleb was cleaning off the baby's face and using the suction tool to clear any aspirated effects from the nostrils and mouth. Once baby began to cry loudly, Caleb placed him into Mrs Sanderson's grateful arms, before clamping the cord.

The midwives began towelling him off, rubbing hard, helping establish breathing and removing wetness so that he didn't get cold.

Rory leaned over to check on the baby and wasn't totally happy with his colour. 'Cord?' she asked.

'Done,' Caleb responded.

'Mrs Sanderson? I just need to take him to check on his breathing. I'll bring him right back to you.' And she scooped up the baby and carried him urgently over to the cot, where the team immediately surrounded him and got to work, placing a small oxygen mask over his face as Rory listened to his chest. 'SATs?'

His result was borderline okay, but they all wanted to make sure he was fine. He might need a chest x-ray to be sure.

'Is he alright?' Mrs Sanderson called out.

Rory turned and smiled. 'I believe so. He might have inhaled a small amount of stool—not enough to cause any serious issues, but we're just monitoring him to make sure his lungs are clear enough. But he's got good colour and he's not grunting so it's looking good. We're just going to keep him on extra oxygen for a while in the Special Care Baby Unit. Remember we discussed that as a possibility?'

Mrs Sanderson nodded, but didn't seem to relax, and Rory knew that she wouldn't until her baby boy was safely back in her arms.

'Let's give Mum a quick cuddle before he goes up,' she ordered.

Caleb scooped up the baby, now wrapped in many blankets, and carefully handed him to his mother. Mrs Sanderson burst into happy tears and kissed her son on the cheeks. 'Declan. His name's Declan.'

'A good, strong name,' Caleb said.

After a few minutes, they took Declan and handed him over to the SCBU team, who whisked him away and told Mrs Sanderson that she could go and visit him when he was properly settled in.

Rory and Caleb left the room and headed to the staff room to write their final notes and then leave for the day.

As she sat at the desk, typing on her tablet, Rory couldn't help but look at Caleb whilst he didn't know he was under observation. He was clearly a good doctor: kind, calm. She wished she could sit there and create a long list of his professional attributes but, annoyingly, all she could really think of as she sat and surreptitiously gazed at him was how handsome he was, how attractive.

She liked the way his dark-brown hair had been cut short on the back and sides but left longer on the top so that it had this kind of ruffled, 'I just got out of bed' look. She could imagine that gorgeous head of hair resting against her pure-white pillows, his beautiful eyes looking at her with mischief in mind. The feel of him in her hand... A wave of arousal washed over her and she felt herself grow hot.

'You know, if you keep staring, I'm going to start thinking that maybe you do want my number. And round two,' he said, smirking.

Rory blinked. 'What?'

'You're staring.'

'I'm not!' she replied, indignant, feeling her cheeks flush with more heat. *How dare he imply that?*

'Yes, you were. And I'm flattered, but Rory, my eyes are up here.' And he laughed and pointed to them, as if she'd not just been thinking about them.

'You're so full of yourself.' She got up and went over to her locker to get her things so she could go and change back into her day clothes, go home and get away from this guy, whose ego was so huge, she was amazed he could make it through doorways.

Seriously, it had been a long day! Having this idiot following her around, making her feel all kind of things, had simply been an extra load she'd not needed. Running into and having to work with her one-night stand? It was embarrassing—and on a day when she was already tired and irritable. She was hungry too, but also not.

She had this strange craving to eat a really fresh, ripe, juicy mango. Just thinking of that made her all flustered, imagining the taste of it and the way the juice would run down her face and neck as she bit into it. She salivated just thinking about it, but also weirdly felt *sick* thinking about it. Her stomach had felt strange all day, and when she'd had lunch earlier her chicken salad had tasted off. She'd thrown half of it away, not wanting to get food poisoning.

'Well, when someone looks at you as much as you have been doing, you begin to wonder if you have something on your face—but I checked and, as there's nothing between my teeth either, I can only presume you keep looking at me because you either can't get enough, or you're intrigued as to why I make you feel a certain way.'

She scoffed. 'Mr Stride! I didn't know you were a psychologist too. Congratulations. Your parents must be proud.'

'My mother is, certainly.'

She stopped, her hand on the doorknob to the changing room. That was the second time he'd implied that he didn't have a great relationship with his father. *Intriguing.* She could certainly understand the principle of a man letting someone down. She'd had enough experience of that to last her a lifetime and she was never going to let it happen again.

She stomped into the changing room and closed the door behind her, feeling incredibly irritated, and wanting to huff and puff and throw things. Instead, she yanked off her scrubs and threw them into the laundry, then pulled on her own clothes from this morning and spent a moment gathering herself, slowing her breathing, before she opened the door to head back out again, hoping that he would already be gone.

But he wasn't. He was sitting there on the couch, chewing on the end of a pen as he stared at his patient's notes. His lips were slightly parted, the tip of his tongue teasing the end of the pen as he thought. She pushed down as much of her arousal as she could, annoyed by it. It was rudely unwanted!

'Goodbye, Mr Stride. I'll no doubt see you to-morrow.'

'Ms Dotson.'

Was it bad to wish that *he* got food poisoning, so he didn't come into work for a few days?

Because he really was the most irritating man she'd ever met!

Over the next few days, Caleb enjoyed his time spent with Rory. It was fun to flirt with her and, even though she didn't seem so amused by it, she seemed to be enjoying it a little, otherwise he'd stop. He wasn't such an ass that he would force himself on anyone—they were just having fun, snatched in the few moments they had when they weren't dealing with patients.

Rory tried to act outraged sometimes; other times, she'd just laugh cynically and say, 'You wish.' And, yes, maybe he did. He would not be opposed to having a bit more fun with the delectable doctor. Their first night had been.

'We should have another night together,' he said one day, as they were standing on the concourse overlooking the large reception area down below.

Rory laughed out loud. 'You're joking?'

'For closure.' He smirked at her. 'I've heard it's a very important thing.'

'Closure, right.'

'And, forgive me for saying it, but you seem a little…uptight. A passionate night of sex might help you unwind, plus I've heard it can do wonders for the complexion.'

She touched her face. 'Are you saying I've got spots?'

'No.' Though, now he'd said it, he noticed that she did have a little breakout. It could be hormonal—some women got that. She'd done her best to cover it with concealer, but as each day wore on it became more obvious.

'You're saying I'm uptight?'

'Oh, most definitely.' He smiled, back on firmer ground. 'You've been wound as tight as a bobbin. I have a few…*techniques* to help with that.'

He gave her a quick glance, smiling, taking in the pallor of her face after a long day, the way a few tendrils of hair had broken free from her pony tail and the dark circles showing under her eyes. But, even with those imperfections, she was still a beautiful, desirable woman to him. One he'd be pleased to have seen upon his arm. One he'd be thrilled to take to his bed.

Their previous night of passion had not been enough. They'd needed to be quick in case they were discovered. It had been abrupt, frenzied and wild and, though he could do that again, his dreams of her lately had involved a more languorous aspect. *Hours*, rather than minutes, in which she would lie naked upon his bed and he would explore every aspect of her. Maybe he'd blindfold her? Trail her skin with a feather…or his *tongue*? Watch her curl and undulate, and listen to her gasps and moans until he tasted the very heart of her? Drive himself deep into her body with his own?

'I'm sure you do,' she answered, smiling back at him. 'But you're going to have to save them for some other lucky girl.'

'Is there someone else you're saving yourself for?' He doubted it. She'd made it pretty obvious that she wasn't in the market for a relationship.

'Not at the moment.'

'Then why not have some fun? Break that one-night rule of yours. Aren't some rules meant to be broken?'

'Some, maybe.' She looked him up and down,

as if considering him, and he could see in her hungry eyes that she liked what she saw. 'But not that one.'

'You're killing me, Rory.'

'Oh! I get it. You have DSB.'

He frowned. 'DSB?'

She leaned in close and whispered, '"Deadly sperm build-up". I've heard most men think it's fatal.' Then she laughed and walked away from him, and all he could do was laugh and watch her go, gaze focused on her hips and the smooth curve of her bottom in her scrubs. Rory filled her scrubs nicely. But he also had a memory of what those curves were like *unrobed* and he wanted to see them again.

He was about to say something else, to have the last word, but both their mobiles went at the same time and they pulled them from their pockets. They were being called to attend an emergency caesarean section.

She looked at him and curled her finger.

CHAPTER FIVE

OKAY. SERIOUS MODE, NOW. Rory didn't look at Caleb as they began to scrub for the surgery. The patient was already in Theatre, gowned and anaesthetised with a spinal. Her husband would be brought in once she and Caleb were ready to go.

It was Natalie Goldberg. They'd been monitoring her during her labour, as she was pregnant with twins. One of them had been showing some decelerations on the CTG tracing for a few hours, and in the last hour it had become significantly worse, according to the midwife who had spoken to them when they arrived at theatre. Mr Atwood-Green, the consultant, had ordered the emergency caesarean, even though Natalie hadn't technically been his patient, but he'd been called in to check the trace because Rory and Caleb had been on their break at the concourse. Now they would take over and hopefully get these babies out before there was a serious threat to their health.

Rory was on high alert now, even though moments ago up on the concourse she'd been feeling tired and exhausted. It was all she felt lately. Probably some vitamin deficiency or something, because she knew she hadn't been eating right lately. She was determined that this weekend she would reset her eating. Maybe she'd batch-cook something, so that she could take some proper meals into work with her. She'd also eat some healthy snacks such nuts or fruit, instead of the sweets she'd been mainlining from the vending machine.

As she headed into Theatre, one of the team helped her on with her gown, tying it behind her, then helping Caleb with his as she got on her gloves and stood over the sterile field of her patient's abdomen.

She took the surgical tweezers and pinched at various parts of the patient's anatomy. 'Feel anything, Natalie?'

'No.'

'Okay, we're going to get started, if you're ready.'

Natalie noddednervously.

Caleb came to stand opposite. 'Scalpel?' She glanced at him once as he took the blade, applied it to the skin and cut the initial incision, then she focused totally on the surgery. He was quick and skilled. He cut through layer after layer with perfection until he exposed the womb, opened it up and began reaching for the first baby. A gush of amniotic fluid burst forth and he had the first twin out in moments.

'Congratulations on Baby A,' he said.

Rory heard Natalie cry as her baby began to wail and she smiled briefly before turning back to watch Caleb retrieve the second baby. The second twin came out a little floppier than the first. It was wet and slick, but the team took him over to the warmer, and pretty soon they heard a second set of lungs join the first, and they all relaxed at the happy sound.

Rory had been feeling so tired, so exhausted, but the sound of the crying babies made that go away briefly. One day, she hoped, she would have the opportunity to have a child of her own. She'd already thought about how she'd do it—alone, through IVF or something—without a guy to let her or her baby down.

Rory glanced up at Caleb, then returned her focus to the incision to assist with the latter part of the surgery: removal of the placentas and stitching the patient back up.

But something else happened. A wave of nausea washed over her as she looked into the open abdomen, and bile rose up in her throat. Rory choked, making a strange, strangled sound as she panic-swallowed it back down and stepped away from the table.

'You okay?' Caleb asked, pausing in his stitching.

'Erm…yeah.' She swallowed again. *What the hell had that been about?* She never got nauseous in Theatre! But in that moment looking at the layers of flesh, muscle and blood had been too much. *Eurgh.* Rory couldn't stand at the table and look. The smell of it all—the amniotic fluid, the blood, the cut flesh, the sheer viscosity and rawness of it—was turning her stomach. She knew she needed to step away or risk vomiting in the body cavity of a patient, which she figured would not be welcomed by the patient, her family or the hospital authorities—though lawyers might be pretty happy about it.

'I, er…need to step away.'

'Okay, go. Get a glass of water; you look a little ashy. Eat some chocolate—get your blood sugars back up.'

She nodded, grateful that he didn't tease her in this moment, in front of everyone. It was bad enough that they were all witnessing this and would no doubt talk about it afterwards. The surgeon who got queasy—that would be a great joke, right? She pulled off her gloves, gown and mask, grateful to breathe easily again, and stepped out of Theatre.

What the hell had just happened to her? Why did she feel so ill all of a sudden? *What did I eat for lunch?* She'd meant to go and get a jacket potato and some salad, just to be healthy, but she'd stuck around for a birth, got called into another case and, somewhere in there, she'd just grabbed a couple of chocolates from the tin on Reception to keep her sugars up. *Damn it, that's why!*

Thankfully, though, it was now home time. Her shift was over and she could go. She would get home, cook something, maybe take a bubble bath and go to bed early. Maybe this nausea would stop once she started taking better care of herself.

After she'd got changed and headed into the staff room, Caleb was waiting for her, looking concerned. 'You okay?'

'Just burning the candle at both ends. I'll be alright once I have something proper to eat at home.'

'What do you have in your fridge?'

She stopped to think and remembered that she'd been working hard all week. She'd not done any shopping. Her expression must have told him everything he needed to know: her shelves would be bare, her fridge, empty.

'Thought so. Listen, let me take you out for a bite to eat.'

She looked at him dubiously.

'As a thank you, for letting me shadow you this week. I know I've been a bit of a thorn in your side.'

'A *bit*?'

He smiled. 'Yeah. A bit. Part of you was charmed, I could tell.'

'Well, Prince Charming, I don't really think I've got the energy to go out to eat. I just want to go home, rest and relax.'

'Then let me cook for you.'

'What?' Was he kidding? Her rules did not allow for her one-night stands not only to start working with her but also come back to hers and start cooking for her.

'Give me your address. You go home, I'll go shop for some real food and then I'll come to your place and cook for you. You won't have to lift a finger.'

It did sound tempting. And, God damn it, she *was* tempted! And exhausted. When had she last had someone take care of her like that—cook for her, shop for her? Even Leo hadn't treated her that way. And would it be so wrong? She'd let a friend do it, if they ever offered, so why not him? All she had to do was not give in to his flirting. 'And what will you be expecting in return for this shopping and cooking experience?'

'Not a thing.' He held up his hands in mock-surrender. 'It's purely a thank you for this week.'

'You're not going to try to seduce me?'

'Not one bit.'

Oh. Is that disappointment I feel? Why the hell am I disappointed? I should feel relieved! 'You can flirt a little bit, if you want. I know you like to.' She gave a grudging smile, as if she were doing *him* a favour.

'Okay. Challenge accepted.'

Rory looked shattered when she answered the door to him, but pale and beautiful in an outfit that made him smile. Clearly she'd put some thought into what outfit would likely be the least sexy to him, but somehow he still thought she looked amazing in it. She wore grey jogging bottoms and an over-sized sweatshirt and her hair was twisted up on top of her head in a messy knot. She wore no make-up.

This was Rory. He could imagine her curled up on the couch looking like this, eating from a tub of ice-cream, licking the spoon as she watched some movie. She was trying to hide her body beneath the over-sized clothes, but it wasn't working, because he already knew what was underneath and it just aroused him even more. To distract himself, he held up the groceries. 'Show me the kitchen.'

He had bought the ingredients for his superfood meal and set about making it: baked sweet potatoes smothered with a spicy chickpea and roast-vegetable stew, drizzled with a light garlic dressing and toasted croutons. They didn't need much. It would be very filling and, as the food cooked, he watched her from his post in the kitchen as she lay on the couch and closed her eyes.

She was beautiful, there was no doubt about it, and there was also an element of vulnerability about her that just pulled at him and made him want to protect her for some reason. There was a blanket over the back of her couch and at one point he draped it over her and watched her sleep for a while before he returned to serve up the food and called out from the kitchen, 'Hope you're hungry!'

He knew that way he could pretend that she hadn't been sleeping, and so could she. She made her way to the small dining table, her face pale and swollen with sleep, and he placed the food in front of her. *'Voilà!'*

'Wow, this looks amazing!'

'Every mouthful will prove to be a scintillating delight.' He smiled, sitting opposite and waiting for her to taste it and give her opinion.

When she did, her reaction was everything he'd wanted it to be: delight, surprise. Deliciousness. Pure wow. 'This is incredible!' she said between hungry mouthfuls. She cleaned the plate in its entirety and he had a sneaky suspicion that, if he'd not been here, then she would have licked it too.

'I, er, have a confession to make,' he said.

She looked at him in suspicion. 'Oh?'

'I may have bought a pre-made, yet decadent, dessert.'

Rory swallowed. 'What kind?'

He got up, went to the fridge and returned with a triple-chocolate mousse in its little pot—milk and white and dark chocolate topped with a chocolate glaze and chocolate sprinkles—and presented it to her with a spoon. 'Got room?'

She smiled wickedly, like a naughty child. 'I have a second stomach reserved purely for desserts like this.'

He watched her devour it—every bite, every spoonful. Every lick of her lips and satisfied moan that he heard her make, turned him on. And all she was doing was eating!

'What?' She looked at him curiously.

'Nothing.'

'No, there's something. Do I have chocolate on my face?'

'No, no, your face is fine. It's more than fine, licking that spoon like that.'

She stopped and blushed, two pink spots filling her pale cheeks. 'Oh. Sorry.'

'No, it's nice. I like it. Do it again,' he said in an amused, low, porn voice.

She put down the spoon and pushed away her plate, irritated. 'Look, you don't want me.'

'No?'

'No.'

'Why?'

'I'm…' She looked away, as if she wasn't sure she wanted to have this conversation. 'I can do fun, Caleb. I can be entertaining for small amounts—it's all I'm good for—but you don't want to know me long-term. I'm not all that interesting.'

'Who says I want to do long-term?'

She smiled sadly.

'Come on. We've already breached your one-night rule. I work with you. I spend time with you on breaks. We laugh. We flirt. We tease. I've cooked for you. Fed you. Tantalised your tastebuds. I would like to think that I tantalised another little bud I can think of.' He grinned. 'We could both scratch that itch we've both been feeling since I walked back into your life. Get it out of our system.'

'You just want to scratch an itch?'

He nodded.

'No strings?'

'Not a single thread.'

He could see she was thinking about it, considering it. He really wanted her to agree to it. It could be fun. It *would* be fun. She was clearly tempted. And what she'd said earlier about him not wanting to know her long-term was nonsense. Why wouldn't he? She was great. *Please say yes. Agree.*

'Okay. But I want a bath first.'

He raised an eyebrow, surprised that she'd agreed. 'I'll run it for you.'

She took her time in the bath, not wanting to rush it, not wanting to seem too eager to join him in the bedroom, even though she was. It was insanity, having a second night with him, knowing that they worked together, that they were colleagues and she would be see him every day after this at the hospital.

But...there was something about him that drew her to him and, now that she'd eaten, rested and washed, she felt amazing. Her tiredness gone, her arousal took first place in her consciousness. She didn't put on any clothes after the bath except for her fluffy bath robe and a dainty anointment of scent from her small collection of perfumes. Then she padded into her bedroom and found him lying on her bed, bare-chested and waiting for her. He looked like a delicious teddy bear with his dark, hairy chest and dark eyes, waiting for her in half-shadow, the cover slightly thrown back.

She thought about what lay beneath the covers—the parts of him she couldn't see. She felt a flush of desire and need, so strong it almost overwhelmed her, to abandon this slow, sultry walk into the bedroom and just pull back the covers, mount him and ride him into the sunset! But she made herself wait, knowing she was wet for him, and turned, slowly undressing by letting the bath robe drop to the floor, and raising her eyes to look at him.

His eyes widened, just as she'd hoped they would, and she watched him run his gaze over her naked body, not for the first time. But this time it felt better. More alluring. More tempting. She felt like some kind of sexy vixen. She was in control of this. *I am.* She had to believe that. It was important to her that all of this was under her control. She crawled into bed alongside him and let him reach out and touch her. Just because she was submitting to his touch did not mean that she was submitting, or submissive. She was the one allowing it. She was the one giving permission to him.

As Caleb pulled her beneath him and began to explore her body, she allowed herself to succumb to the masterful sensations he was creating. It had been a long time since she'd made love to a man in a bed. After Leo, all her previous encounters had been quickies. An abandoned hotel function room… The one before that had been in the back seat of a car—not as sexy as it appeared in films or on television. The one before that had taken place in a bathroom of a friend's house on New Year's Eve.

Before that, it had been Leo—her ex-fiancé and

her first, and only, true love. A man she'd thought she'd be with for ever! A man to whom she had given her whole heart, believing that he would treasure it. A man who had hauntingly humiliated her in front of everyone she knew—every friend, every family member. A man whom she had subsequently discovered had been cheating on her. Since that day, she had refused to let any man have power over her, ever again.

But Caleb? He was not like those others. He was a real man. A solid, well-muscled, well-built and well-hung man who was now causing her to gasp and catch her breath as he explored her body with his tongue and his expert hands. The man could handle a scalpel, that was for sure, but he also knew intimately what to do with the rest of him, and it felt so good!

She wanted to lie there for ever and just let him do whatever he wanted, but she was not a passive player when it came to sex, so when she felt like she couldn't take any more she rolled him over and began to show him what *she* could do.

Together they tumbled, rolled, gasped and came and, after a rest, they did it all over again, and a third time, before falling asleep together, exhausted, sated and feeling that it was a draw. She didn't mean to fall asleep in his arms, but he was so warm, his body felt so right, she was so tired and so it just happened. Her head lay on his chest, her fingers mid-twirl in his chest hair. She was soothed to exhausted sleep by his heartbeat.

She had very sweet dreams that night.

The real nightmare began when she woke up.

CHAPTER SIX

WHEN SHE WOKE, she was still wrapped in his arms, warm, cosy and content. If she'd been a cat, she would have purred. She'd never slept over with anyone except Leo, so to find herself now in another man's arms was a pleasant surprise. She had slept so well. Her body felt sated, her body felt… *Okay, why does my stomach feel off?*

Behind her, Caleb still slept peacefully. She shifted slightly, propping herself up onto one elbow and turned and looked at him. If she'd felt her normal self, she would have ravished him again, as he looked so delicious just lying there, but she was beginning to feel quite sick. Had she eaten too much last night? Maybe the dessert had been too sweet.

I need to drink some water or something.

Carefully, she unwrapped herself from his embrace, grabbed her robe from off the floor and made her way to the landing. Her intention was to reach the kitchen, grab a glass of water and maybe put on the kettle on and make a coffee or something. Maybe eat some dry toast and hope that that settled her. But she never made it that far. As she crept away from her room, bile rose up suddenly into her throat and she rushed to the bathroom and was sick. She tried to be as quiet as he could, not wanting to wake Caleb, not wanting to let him know that she was ill.

When it was over, she wiped her mouth, washed it out with water and gazed up at her reflection in the mirror. She was pale again, exhausted again—now sick. If she didn't know any better, she'd say she was pregnant, but that was impossible, right? When could that have…?

She turned to look towards the direction of the bedroom, where Caleb slept. Her last sexual encounter had been with him, but they'd used protection, and besides she had polycystic ovarian syndrome; she'd been told the likelihood of her getting pregnant on her own was going to be difficult.

Not impossible, though—just difficult. She'd not checked the condom, nor had he. She'd simply taken it from him in that dark room, wrapped it in tissue and disposed of it. What if it had split? What if, right now, she was standing here incubating an embryo?

Heat washed over her and she began to sweat profusely. It all made sense! The exhaustion, the weird cravings, the nausea, the way food tasted off, the odd taste in her mouth… Had her body been sending her signals all this time and she'd dismissed them because she'd been busy or thought it an impossibility?

I need to know for sure.

One thing she did know was that she couldn't tell *him*. Not yet. Not until she was certain, and then she'd decide what to do. Until she knew, she would have to act normal. They had slept together again. It had been an amazing night, but now they had to work together, and this was not a relationship. Neither of them had committed to anything, except agreeing on no-strings-at-all sex. As far as she was aware, 'no strings' usually meant no request from one party to the other that they suddenly become a daddy and play happy families.

Why is this happening to me?

Caleb woke in Rory's bed feeling refreshed and happy. He'd had a great night with a fabulous woman, and he was looking forward to getting something to eat to refill his engine before they started a long day at work together.

But first things first—where was she? He would love to have woken with her in his arms and enjoy a little snuggle before they both got up, showered and dressed. Maybe they could share a shower. The idea of Rory and him standing under some steamy water whilst he soaped up her body appealed to him greatly. But she was already gone. Maybe she was just an early riser. He was, generally. If he'd been at home, he might even have gone for a run. Just a mile or two, to really wake him up and get himself mentally ready for the day.

The bed smelt of her, of sex. He pulled her pillow to his face and inhaled, breathing in the scent of her hair and perfume, before he let it go, swung his naked body from the bed and dressed in the clothes he'd been wearing yesterday. He had a spare set in his car, so he could get changed into a new shirt and tie before he returned to work. No-one would know that they had spent the night together, which was probably how they would both like it.

Hearing sounds filtering from the kitchen, and inhaling the scent of brewing coffee, he made his way there, standing in the doorway, still buttoning up his shirt as he watched Rory clear up their plates from the night before, which had been forgotten. 'Good morning.'

She jumped at the sound of his voice and glanced at him.

'Forget I was here?' he asked with a smile. He'd like to think that he wasn't forgettable. Last night was most certainly not a night he would forget in a hurry. It was a night in which amazing memories had been made and he would cherish them for a long time.

'Of course not. I just didn't hear you get up. Coffee?'

'Please.'

She grabbed a mug and poured him some, passing it over.

'Are you not having one?'

'No, I, er...fancy some juice.' She pulled open the fridge, poured herself a glass of fresh orange juice and took a small sip, pausing afterwards, as if she was checking something, before putting it down and carrying on with the tidying up.

'Let me help you.'

'It's fine.'

'Hey, I made this mess, let me help you clear it up.'

She sighed and stood back, letting him gather things, scrape plates and rinse them before they went into the dishwasher. 'Breakfast?' she asked.

'Whatever you're having is fine.'

'Oh, I was just going to have some toast.... You probably want something a bit more filling.' She checked in the fridge again, but it was appallingly empty except for a questionable pack of pancetta that sat at the back that he'd noticed was out of date when he'd put his food shopping in there yesterday evening. 'I have bacon, if you want me to fry that?' But she didn't sound like she wanted to at all.

Perhaps he had already outstayed his welcome by staying over. Perhaps she'd thought that, after the no-strings sex, he would escape her bed and go home. Perhaps she was embarrassed by this morning conversation. 'Want me to go?' he offered, trying to be a gentleman.

She turned and looked at him, hope filling her eyes. 'That might be best. You'll want to change clothes, I'm guessing, before work.'

Right. She was embarrassed. 'Aren't you worried the neighbours might talk, seeing a handsome man leave your place so early in the morning?'

'I barely know them.'

He'd hoped for a little protest, but clearly she wanted him gone. It stung a little, but it was probably better that way. He didn't want to look as though he was hoping for more here. This encounter was no strings. 'Okay, then. I'll go.'

She smiled. 'Okay.'

'But we're good? It's not going to be awkward at work?' he pressed. He didn't like awkwardness. He liked niceness. He liked flirtatiousness. He liked working with her.

'We're good.'

'Alright.' He took one final slurp of his coffee, put down his mug and then went over to her to kiss her one last time. He couldn't resist. She seemed taken aback, but accepted the kiss and tried her best to not look uncomfortable afterwards. Did he have morning breath? Surely he should have just tasted of coffee? That wasn't bad, was it? She must drink it, as she had it in the house, along with the coffee machine. Or maybe it was just the extended stay. He was meant to have gone and perhaps she just wasn't a morning person. 'I'll see you at work.'

'Yes. See you.'

He grabbed his jacket and left, heading out to his car in the crisp morning air and congratulating himself on giving her a good time. Rory had been everything he had felt she would be. They'd had quick sex, slow sex, passionate sex. They'd had it all and she'd been just as hungry for him as he'd been for her. But they'd scratched that itch between them now and they could just get on with work. It wouldn't stop him from flirting with her, though, because it had been *so fine*.

Maybe they could continue with their no-strings relationship. It would certainly suit him and he most decidedly hoped it would suit her too.

Rory slipped into the ultrasound room unnoticed and locked the door from the inside, switching on the equipment. Her heart was pounding, her blood pulsing in her ears.

She'd bought a pregnancy testing-kit from a

chemist on the way in and had slipped into the first bathroom stall she'd found. Her hands had shaken as she'd opened the small package and read the instructions, telling herself that she was being ridiculous even testing; there had to be another reason for her symptoms. One last voice had pleaded for reason in a world that was filled with insanity. She'd peed on the stick, placed the test on the the cistern and waited, trying to ignore her churning stomach, trying to ignore the chatter she heard from other visitors to the bathroom. Eventually, she had picked up the test to look at it, but her hands had been trembling so much, the test had slipped from her fingers and fallen into the toilet bowl.

'No!' she'd cried out, staring at it lying there, submerged on the bottom, the test result unseen.

She'd dithered for a moment, then plunged her hand into the cold water, grimacing as she reached for the test and pulled it out to see two pink lines. But was that because of her, or because of the previous visitor to the toilet? There'd been no time to run back out to the chemist, and she wasn't sure she wanted to spend another ten pounds on something she might drop, so that had only left her with one option: the ultrasound room.

She couldn't do a blood test. If she ran a test under her own name testing for HCG, people would know. Even if she ran it under Jane Doe the staff would ask questions as to who was this mystery patient. So this was the only other way. No-one would think anything of an obstetric doctor going into the ultrasound room. This way, scanning herself, she would know for sure without anyone having to run a test and make her wait for an answer.

It was the not knowing that was awful. Her mind was going everywhere. What she would do if it was positive? How to tell *him*? How to tell everyone that she'd allowed herself to get knocked up when she was an obstetrician and ought to know better? When they were *both* obstetric surgeons!

She turned the monitor so that she'd be able to see it from the bed and placed the ultrasound wand down whilst she lowered her scrubs and squirted some cold gel onto her lower abdomen. Was it her imagination, or did it look rounder, already?

No. Impossible. If there is a baby in there, I'd only be a few weeks—classed as two months, maybe? Her cycle was all over the place from her PCOS, so she could only estimate, but she'd slept with Caleb nearly two months ago now...

Rory grabbed the wand and sucked in a steadying breath before she applied it to her abdomen and moved it around until the screen showed her the black space that was her womb…and there, at the bottom, a bean-shaped embryo, a tiny flicker in its chest.

Oh my God!

She almost dropped the transponder device and, as she did so, her hand jerked and something else flashed up on the screen. She blinked, not sure if she'd seen right. This time she moved it more slowly, wishing she'd done this standing up so that she could use the buttons on the machine for more detail, but…yes. There it was.

A second bean.

A second flicker.

Two babies. Two.

Twins.

This can't be! How was this happening? How was she pregnant with not one baby, but two? They weren't even in a proper relationship! She'd always assumed, because of the PCOS, that she would have to accept a surrogate. Or adopt. Or go through long rounds of IVF. That having a baby, having a family, would be expensive, hard and difficult to achieve. That she would have to go through lots of paperwork and heartache before it happened. Leo had never wanted to stick around to wait, though. He'd found someone else. Someone more fun, more spontaneous. He said she'd got too serious.

Caleb wasn't in the market to have a *relation-*

ship. He enjoyed no-strings fun, like her. That was it. That was the extent of their relationship, if you could call it that. They were friends and colleagues with benefits at this point, nothing more. She couldn't rely on him to be there for her, so she was already willing to go it alone.

She moved the scanner again and tried to find the one detail she wanted to see, but it wasn't there. There was no line between the twins indicating that they were in separate sacs. And she could only see one placenta—which meant identical twins. And it also meant that carrying these babies could come with a whole load of extra problems she didn't need.

'Hey, there you are! I've been looking for you all morning,' Caleb said when he finally saw Rory emerge from the lift onto the Maternity floor.

'Oh, yeah, I've been busy.' She tried to walk past him, holding a file in front of her stomach.

'Rory, wait.'

She stopped and turned to face him, eyes wary. 'What is it?'

He stepped up close. Close enough that they could have a private conversation, but not so close that people might think they were intimate. 'We're okay, right? After last night?'

They had to be. He really wanted to keep a good thing going with her, because the two of them together were sexual dynamite. And, to put the cherry on the cake too, he really liked her as a person. Respected her and the fact that she knew what she wanted from life and wasn't afraid to ask for it.

'Sure.' She looked away, around them, making sure no-one could hear.

Did he believe her? Right now, no, he didn't. 'Look, let's meet for lunch. I've got a case right now, but I should be free about one-thirty.'

'I'm kinda busy to be honest with you, Caleb.'

'Please.' He gave her the look. A look that he had carefully cultivated over many years to be earnest and innocent. A 'please trust me' look. A 'please help me' look. A 'I don't mean any harm' look. He'd created it to use on his sisters. Being the only boy and the youngest of four kids, he'd often felt outnumbered by them, left out by them. And, with no dad around, he'd often felt desperate for company and for someone to talk to. Though he'd not dusted it off for decades, he was able to bring it out now and use it to perfection, because she finally caved and nodded.

'Okay. One-thirty.'

He smiled in triumph as she walked off, having got his way, his gaze focusing on the lovely way those scrubs moulded her body. A body that he had again become intimately acquainted with last night. If anything, she'd looked even more amazing than he remembered from the first time. The first time, he'd gone mostly by touch—when she had allowed it—and used his imagination. But last night he'd seen and felt everything, and she'd been so beautiful, so curvy, he'd almost exploded with his desire to consume everything about her: the swell of her hips, the curve of her bottom, her full, large breasts that had seemed so responsive to his touch. She'd tasted amazing and those little sounds she'd made before she'd orgasmed, the gasps as it had built up, had been just as delightful as the orgasm itself.

When she turned the corner and went out of sight, he headed off to check on his patient. The midwife looking after her thought that maybe she was showing signs of pre-eclampsia, a condition that could be extremely dangerous to the mother and baby, resulting in high blood pressure, severe headache, nausea, vomiting and even in full eclampsia or fitting. This patient was considered high risk. She was forty-two years of age and carrying twins, and had been advised to take aspirin since about twelve weeks, but the midwife reported that the labouring mother was experiencing intense headaches and was showing protein in her urine.

'Hi, Daphne, my name's Mr Stride. Morgan has called me in to talk to you about your results.'

Daphne sat and listened to him as best she

could whilst having her contractions, but she was struggling. Her headache was bad, her blood pressure was rising and he didn't like what he saw on the CTG machine. The babies showed signs of not being happy in utero.

'In this situation, with the threat of pre-eclampsia, the only thing to help it is to deliver the babies. Normally, I would be happy to give you some medication to increase your contractions and get this baby delivered vaginally. But, as you're having twins, we don't need the complications of delivering one and then having problems getting baby number two out. With your permission, I'd like to suggest we take you down to Theatre and deliver the babies by caesarean section.'

Daphne finished breathing through her contraction and looked up at him, red-faced and sweating. 'Do what you have to do to get them here safe.'

'Alright. We'll get you to Theatre.'

He instructed Morgan and then left the room to call down to the theatres, telling them to prepare for a twin delivery. Daphne was at thirty-seven weeks, so he didn't expect the twins to need too much help after delivery, but he would still have the SCBU team there just in case.

Rory sat nursing a cup of cooling tea in the hospital cafeteria She'd also bought a chicken-salad wrap, along with a small plate of fries, figuring she needed to eat better now that she was eating for three. Three!

My life is crazy right now.

But every time she tried to take a bite of food her stomach lurched in protest. Pre-scan, she'd been able to try and eat the food, but *post-scan*? Now that she knew for sure that she was pregnant, it was like her body had fully acknowledged the morning sickness and was saying *this food will make you sick.*

She knew it wasn't just the food making her feel she couldn't take a bite. It was the knowledge. The knowledge that she was pregnant with two babies. She was in shock, her stomach in turmoil.

It lurched again when she saw Caleb walking towards her carrying a tray, and she managed a weak smile when he slid into the booth opposite her. He had a cup of coffee and a portion of lasagne with a side of broccoli, and the aroma of his food, the sight of it, made her want to hurl. She swallowed the feeling down.

'So…twins!' he said, beaming.

Rory stared at him. *'Wh…what?'*

'I've added two more to my delivery total. A healthy set of bouncing baby boys! Mind you, it was risky there for a moment,' he said, unrolling his knife and fork from the serviette and diving into the lasagne, unaware of the look of relief that spread across her face.

'That's great,' she managed.

She could not tell him about the pregnancy just yet. It was still early days. As an obstetrician, she knew that anything could happen in the first trimester. She could lose the pregnancy, miscarry the twins, and why tell him if that was going to happen? Probably best to keep this to herself until she got past the first twelve weeks.

'Multiples are always such a worry, aren't they?'

'I guess they can be,' she answered, thinking about two cots, two car seats, two lots of nappies, two screaming babies...

'And then, when the delivery is over and they're safe, you can finally breathe again. I'm not saying singleton pregnancies don't worry you as much, but twins and triplets and quadruplets and quintuplets...' He laughed. 'They scare the hell out of you more. Have you ever delivered quintuplets?'

She shook her head. 'No. Triplets a couple of times, but nothing more than that. You?'

'I saw a set of quadruplets born. I was involved in the case over in San Diego. The mother had had IVF and implanted two fertilised eggs and they both split. She carried them to thirty weeks and delivered two boys and two girls. They always send me a Christmas card.'

She managed a smile.

'Not hungry?' he asked, pointing at her un-touched food.

'No, I, er…grabbed a snack earlier and kind of spoilt my appetite,' she lied, hating lying to him, but knowing that she could not give him any inkling as to what was going on with her. This was her burden and hers alone, right now. If she got past twelve weeks, then he could carry it with her, and she would just have to hope beyond hope that he would do the decent thing and stand by her and support her.

I guess I need to know more about what kind of guy he is.

'Caleb, can I ask you something?'

'Sure,' he answered, forking in a mouthful of broccoli.

'Do you…like babies?'

He looked puzzled at her question and laughed. 'What kind of weird question is that? Course I do!'

'You always wanted to be an obstetrician?'

Caleb nodded. 'Yes.'

'Even before you did placements in your training?'

Another nod. 'Yes. There were two very strong reasons as to why I wanted to be an obstetrician.'

'Care to share?'

He smiled. 'Alright. I'll play the game of you

wanting to get to know the man you've shared a bed with for *two* nights. Not one. I mean, there had to be something special about me, right?' He winked at her. 'Okay, the first reason. My dad was a cardiologist, and he assumed I would be a cardiologist like him, and so I knew I had to pick something other than cardiology because I didn't want to be anything like him. I look like him, I sound like him, I even have his blood type, but I was not going to be his mini-me.'

'Why not?'

Caleb gave a short laugh. 'If you knew him, you wouldn't have to ask.'

'Daddy issues. Okay.' Father issues was a red flag. It probably meant that Caleb wouldn't make a great father either, until he worked to resolve his issues. She'd like to think that he would be great, but her past experiences with men abandoning her and going after someone better told her that this would probably be the same. 'And the second reason?'

'My mum.'

Of course. 'Because you were premature?'

He nodded. Rory stared at him, hoping he'd say more, reveal more.

'My mum went through a tough time, and she told me about it when I was old enough to know. She was scared. All her other pregnancies with my sisters had been fine, but with me she got to twenty-nine weeks and boom—started contractions. She had an infection, and she was scared and going into early labour, and no-one could tell her if I would be strong enough to survive back then. My dad got called to a patient and left her on her own, and so she turned to the staff to keep her calm and comforted. And they were there for her through it all, even when she nearly died. I wanted to be able to do that for someone else, if I could. Pay it forward.'

'She nearly died?' That sounded terrifying.

'The infection in her body was overwhelming and she'd become septic. Thankfully, they managed to save her. And me. They sat by our beds when my father didn't.'

Rory wasn't sure she could do this alone. What if something like that happened to her? Who would sit by her bed and pray for her? Maylee? Her mother? Caleb? And if everything did go okay... One baby was hard enough, but two—how would she deal with two? She would have to stop working! She would have to give her life over to two very demanding children; her life would never be the same again!

'What about you? Why did you become an obstetrician?' he asked her.

'Oh. I, er, wasn't sure what kind of doctor I wanted to be. But my first placement as a medical student was in labour and delivery and I became enamoured of it: the happy stories; the joy; watching people become a family. I know there are a few sad cases, but they're outnumbered by the good, aren't they?' she asked him, wanting to know his answer, thinking about the identical twins she carried.

She knew the risks, the possible issues with twin-to-twin transfusion syndrome when one twin got more of the blood supply and grew bigger, whereas the other one stayed small. Both twins were at risk; even though one would think the bigger twin would therefore be stronger, it wasn't always that way.

Rory had never thought she would end up with a problem pregnancy, because she'd never thought she'd be able to get pregnant anyway! But she couldn't end this pregnancy. It was a miracle, even if it was unexpected, a shock and not something she'd planned. Whatever fate had in store for her, she had to face it. And this was not like the aftermath of Leo's shock decision; this was hers to make and deal with. And, if everything went well this first trimester, Caleb's too.

'Have you ever thought of becoming a father?' she asked him, the question coming from her lips without her thinking about it.

'Me? Hah! I don't think I'd make a good father, and there is no way I'd want to be anything like mine, so…most likely not. Don't get me wrong, I love kids—I love babies and seeing them make other people happy is great—but as long as I can hand them over to someone else at the end of the day, then that's enough for me. I can live vicariously through them.'

Oh. Right. Yeah, the daddy issues. I kind of knew about those.

But it hurt to hear him say it. To hear him say that he wouldn't make a good father, so he'd rather not try.

Well, Caleb, you might just not have any choice in the matter—like me.

Over the next few weeks, Caleb began to notice how Rory kept finding the opportunity to sit down with him and ask him questions about his life. She was very curious! But she kept asking the questions he'd expect from someone who was aiming to be his girlfriend, and that put him on the back foot. So he instinctively did what he felt was right and tried to paint himself as the most dysfunctional person ever, with a terribly broken family, as much as he could aiming to make himself appear as someone with whom she would not want to form a long-term emotional attachment. Because he was good at putting up the barriers. It not only kept him safe, but her too. There was a nice line between enjoying sex with someone and being in a romantic relationship and he knew not to overstep it.

He continued to flirt, as he always did, but she seemed to be holding him at arm's length physically. He kind of liked the hot and cold nature of it, because it was almost like a game—which Rory would he get? And could he be persuasive enough to get her to let him back into her bed, despite him being supposedly dysfunctional?

He dreamed of her, if he was honest. Those two nights with her were very pleasant memories indeed and, though he was not in the market for a relationship, he had to admit that if he were it would be with someone like her. She was beautiful, talented, clever, skilled and sexy. She was fun in bed, fun at work. She made him smile, laugh and feel warm inside. She made him feel that he *mattered*. That was rare, and confusing, because he had to keep reminding himself that they were not going out, nor did either of them want that.

'Your father's in town,' his mother said to him on the phone, as he stood on the concourse during a break between patients.

'And that would be important to me why?'

'He asked to meet with me, to put me in the picture.'

'What picture is that?'

'He's moving back to London.'

'With Ella? And the kids?' Ella was his father's

second wife. His second attempt at being a good husband and a good family man. He'd had two more babies with Ella, Caleb's half-siblings, but they'd never met.

'Alone. He and Ella broke up, and he met up with me to say he thinks he made a mistake and wants me back.'

Caleb's mouth dropped open. 'You're joking!' *More dysfunction to add to his family back story if Rory asked.*

'No.'

'And what did you say?'

'I told him that I would always love him, because he is the father of my children, but that I could never put myself back in a situation where I was not as important to him as his job or his patients.'

'And what did he say?'

'That he'd changed. That he'd been having therapy and that he wanted to make things right, with you and the girls too.'

'Right. Yeah, he left one family to make another, and when that didn't work out left *them* too. Sounds like a decent guy. Jeez, what did you ever see in him, Mum?'

'I loved him and people do crazy things when they're in love.'

He became aware of movement at his side and realised Rory was standing beside him. She must have just arrived. He gave her a smile and raised a finger to let her know he'd be a moment. 'Further evidence as to why you will never find me falling in love. Which hospital is he working at? Just so I know to never go there.'

'I'm not sure. I didn't ask.'

'Oh, well, when you find out let me know. You'd think a cardiologist would have more sense about the human heart.'

His mum laughed. 'You would. He asked if your number is still the same. It's up to you if you answer him or not. Anyway, I'd better let you go. Take care, honey, and I'll see you soon.'

He wouldn't answer. His dad had had enough chances. 'Okay. Bye bye.' He ended the call. 'Hey.' He turned to smile at Rory.

'Hey. Who were you talking to?'

'My mum. Apparently my dad is back in town, alone and wanting a reconciliation.'

'Oh! And that's…bad?'

'Yes! The guy can't commit to anything, unless it's a patient and they're under anaesthetic; then the man can give his all. But if you're anyone else… Did you know that when I was seven years old I developed appendicitis?'

'No, I don't think you've told me that.'

'I'd been to a friend's birthday party and I developed tummy ache. My mum thought that maybe I'd eaten too many sweets and cakes, but overnight I got really bad and started throwing up and became feverish. Dad was at the hospital doing a night shift, and she called him to tell him she was taking me to A&E. My appendix had burst and I had to go into surgery. Guess how many times he visited me?'

'Er…once?'

'Try never.'

'What?' She looked shocked.

'He told my mum that appendicitis was a common surgery and nothing to worry about and that I'd be fine. And I was, but he didn't even come to see me once, because he got the chance to scrub into a heart transplant instead. My mother never forgave him for that and neither did I. He's always been the same way. A tragically distant dad, which is why you will never find me becoming one!'

'I'm sorry,' she said, her voice low.

'Why? It's not your fault he was a screw-up.'

'He hurt you. Doesn't mean you'd be the same way.'

Caleb shrugged. 'I'll never take that chance. I got used to not being important enough.'

'Maybe that's another reason you became a doctor—to become important. To feel like you mattered.'

He smiled at her. She was always trying to psychoanalyse him lately. It was cute! 'Maybe you should have gone into mental health services. You'd be good at it.'

'No thanks. I love the job I have.'

'Good. Because you're amazing at it.'

'Thank you.'

'Did you, er, need me for something? Because I'm available if you're looking for someone to rock your world in a linen cupboard or anything like that.' He winked.

Rory smiled. 'I do need you, but not for that, sadly.'

'Sadly is right.' He let out a dramatic sigh.

'But I do need you to cover for me for an hour tomorrow. I have an appointment that I can't miss.'

'Tomorrow? What time?'

'Nine o'clock. I know you're not on until the afternoon, but if you cover for me then I'll cover for you later and you could go home early.'

'Sure. Everything alright?'

'Why wouldn't everything be alright?'

He shrugged. 'No reason.'

'So you'll do it?'

'Sure. Now have you really given enough thought to what I said about the linen cupboard?'

Rory smirked and walked away.

He watched her go. The woman got curvier and curvier with every day. Or maybe it was just his eyesight appreciating the view, or his brain letting him see more about her, the more he knew. Whatever it was, he liked it very much indeed.

CHAPTER SEVEN

RORY HAD BEEN TO see her GP. She'd had the pregnancy confirmed, had registered with a midwife and, because she'd told the doctor it was twins from having scanned herself, the doctor had arranged for Rory to be scanned properly so that measurements could be taken and the pregnancy carefully assessed. 'I don't doubt your own skills and abilities, but we need to do this right,' Dr Staedtler had said. And so the text had come through to say that, though it was last minute, there was an available slot tomorrow morning for a scan of the babies.

Rory knew she ought to have contacted her GP earlier, but she'd been in shock for a while, getting used to the idea of carrying twins, and then she'd waited to see if anything would go wrong, which she'd been convinced it would. But when she kept waking up, still pregnant and still nauseous, she'd made an appointment and got it sorted.

No more sticking her head in the sand. She had to do this right! She'd started taking pre-natal vitamins such as folic acid as soon as she found out. Now she sat in the ultrasound department of a neighbouring hospital to St Henry's, because she'd not wanted Caleb or anyone else to see her name in the system and know before she was ready to tell them.

The other women in the waiting room seemed to be calmly excited. She wondered how many of them sitting there today were there because they'd had sex with a stranger and ended up with more than they were bargaining for. *Probably only me*. She assumed that the others were all happily married, or in committed relationships. She assumed they had a supportive partner, even though, through her own work, she knew the odds of that probably weren't accurate. She saw lots of women come through her department doing it on their own, and with every single one she'd thought about how brave they were and how strong.

Funny how she didn't feel that way herself. There was nothing brave about her right now: she was terrified of what this would mean, trying to parent two babies on her own. Would she have to give up her job? Maybe she'd have to try to wrangle support from a guy, who though sexy as hell, was not going to be father of the year, because he'd already made it quite plain that being a father was the furthest thing from his mind.

A couple of the mothers had toddlers with

them. She watched the little ones play, toddling around the chairs and drooling. One touched her skirt with a particularly sticky hand and she smiled politely despite the mother's apologies. Would that be her soon? But, having two, what if they ran off in opposite directions? Which one would she go after? How would she choose? Rory felt sick for a moment, then her name was called and she went into the room with the sonographer, who introduced herself and told Rory to lie on the couch and loosen and lower her waistband.

Rory was about eleven weeks now and she'd already noticed things getting tight. She'd already gone up a size in scrubs, because she wanted— needed—them to look baggy to hide her growing bump. After today, she'd have a better idea of how everything was going—if the babies were growing appropriately, what might be her risks for certain conditions and her schedule for future checks. But it also meant that after this appointment she would have to start telling people: her mum; Maylee.

Caleb.

She'd tried to imagine it. She'd practised the conversation with him over and over again in her mind, trying out different reaction scenarios. In one, Caleb was amazing and kind and, though shocked, he would be happy to try and be there for her as much as she needed. That was the conversation she liked practising the most. But the one that haunted her was the one in which he looked at her in abject shock and horror and told her that he'd support her financially, but that was all, reminding her of all the times he'd told her that he could never be a father.

'Any history of multiples in the family?' the technician asked.

'No. Not that I'm aware.'

'Well, these are definitely identical twins, but they look great to me at the moment. Measuring their thigh length and head circumference, they're both the size I'd expect to see in normal singleton pregnancies.'

'That's good.'

The technician nodded. 'It's very good. We'll keep track of their measurements with each scan so we can measure their growth along the percentile scale.'

The percentile scale was a way to measure a baby's growth by comparing their measurements to other babies of the same gestation, age and gender. So, if a baby was on the fiftieth percentile for weight, then they were right in the middle and average. If a baby was on the ninetieth percentile, then that baby was weighing more than ninety percent of other babies of the same gestation, age and gender.

'This is Baby A's heart.'

Rory heard and monitored babies' heartbeats every day in her work. But hearing her own child's heartbeat had a broad smile crossing her face at the exact same time her eyes filled with happy tears. She'd not expected such a reaction from herself, but she'd noted of late just how emotional she'd been getting as her body filled with extra hormones.

They listened to both babies' hearts and she cried for each one. The technician told her that the babies were measuring at twelve weeks and one day's gestation.

'Everything looks great. Would you like pictures?'

Rory nodded numbly and sat up, wiping the gel from her abdomen and doing up her skirt. The babies were well and healthy. So was she. There was no reason to keep this news from anyone any more. She wished…part of her wished…that Caleb could have been here to see this. To share in this. By not telling him earlier, she had stopped him from having the chance and now she felt guilty and sad. Would she always do this alone? Probably. Caleb wasn't a good bet for a father.

But the pictures the technician passed her were enough to lift her heart again, and she thanked her and left. She had to get to work.

And she had to tell Caleb that his greatest fear was coming true.

* * *

Caleb had just performed a caesarean on a woman who had failed to progress. He hated that term— as if it was her fault or something, when she had no control over how strong or frequent her contractions were, or how much she could dilate. The baby's heart had begun to show consistent decelerations and the decision had been made by the parents and the team to intervene for the sake of the mother, who was exhausted, and for the baby.

It had been a good outcome and a wise one. The cord had been wrapped multiple times around the baby's neck and a vaginal delivery might have proved incredibly risky for its health. Instead, they had a happy mother and a happy baby, and that was all that mattered.

So he felt on top of the world when he emerged from Theatre and found Rory waiting for him. 'Hey! How's it going?'

'Mmm…good.' She looked apprehensive, as if she wanted to ask him out or something. Maybe she did. He perked up even more and gave her his best smile. 'Could I ask you to meet me for lunch in the hospital canteen?'

'Sure, no problem. What time?'

'Erm…about one? One-thirty, maybe?'

'Of course! I wouldn't miss it.' She had very quickly become one of his favourite people to hang around with in the few short months he'd been working here.

'Great. I'll see you later, then.'

She gave him a weird look before she walked away, and he felt his pulse thrum within his veins. Did she want to suggest that, after all these weeks of flirting, they take their relationship to the next level? Because he would happily meet up with her for intimate relations any time she wanted!

Being friends with benefits with Rory would be amazing and perfect—just what he was looking for. She was a wild cat in bed, and he'd loved every moment of being with her, which was why he'd constantly tried to score a repeat of that second night. And besides, he'd liked spooning her all night. He could most definitely see them both doing more of that. He was a very sexual being, and he felt she was too.

If only she'd allow them both free rein to continue to enjoy the adult fun they had experienced together so far. They'd proved that they could do that and still work well together, so what would be the issue? Nothing he could see. And if they kept it all about sex then there was no danger of either of them thinking that it was going to become something more—though, he had to admit to himself, if he were to pick someone with whom to be in a relationship, she was the kind of woman he'd choose.

When lunch time arrived, he headed up to the canteen, hungry for many things. He scanned the crowd and saw her seated at a booth near the back. He gave her a quick wave, grabbed a chicken Caesar wrap and a cup of tea and headed over to their table.

She had an empty soup bowl in front of her and a side plate of crumbs, from which he figured she'd had a bread roll or two. 'You need to eat more than that,' he said, knowing how busy and hectic their jobs were. They needed energy to sustain themselves as doctors, on their feet all day *and* performing surgeries. They couldn't allow their blood sugar to drop for a moment. And, if they were going to take part in extra-curricular activities in linen closets, then she'd definitely need to keep up her energy levels.

'I'll grab dessert in a minute. I wanted to talk to you first.'

'Okay. What's up? Oh, how did your thing go this morning?'

She smiled and nodded. 'Good. Actually, it's… kind of what I wanted to talk to you about.'

He was intrigued. 'Okay. Shoot.' He bit into his wrap hungrily.

'I've er…kind of been unsure lately about whether to tell you something, but after this morning I know that I can't hold it back any longer. And, whether you like it or not, you need to know something.'

Know something? His smile faltered. Oh. Had she fallen for him? Was that why she'd been blowing hot and cold? Was she struggling with her own feelings for him? Because if that was what had happened here then, despite their chemistry, he was going to have to let her down gently.

'I had a hospital appointment this morning. At Guy's.'

Okay. This was not what he'd expected to hear. A hospital appointment at Guy's? He swallowed his mouthful of food and frowned. He felt a little worried for her, a little concerned. What did this have to do with him? Unless, of course… *Ah*. The *only* reason she'd go to another hospital would be so that she didn't have a patient record here. It had to be something she was embarrassed about. But he'd not noticed any weird or worrying symptoms of his own, so he didn't think that she'd passed anything onto him, if that was what she was worried about.

'Hey, it's okay. *I'm fine*,' he said, trying to reassure her.

'*What?*'

'I don't have anything and I regularly screen if I have a new partner—which, admittedly, isn't that often. Are you okay?'

She looked a little confused and annoyed, and

she shook her head. 'No, Caleb, I'm not talking about an STD here!' she said, low and urgently.

'Then what are you talking about?'

'I'm trying to tell you that I'm pregnant! With your baby! Well, with a little more than that, actually. With *both* your babies.'

He couldn't be hearing her right. She was *pregnant*. Both babies…? Did she mean she was pregnant with twins? *'What?'*

'I'm twelve weeks' pregnant.' She paused to scan his face then slid a picture across the table. 'Congratulations.'

What she said couldn't be right. This had to be a joke. They'd used contraception. He remembered her asking for it that first night in the room they'd sneaked off to when they'd had sex. He'd removed the condom and…he'd not checked it. He'd passed it to her and she'd placed it in a tissue and said she'd get rid of it. It had been dark; he'd not thought to check it. Had it burst? Because they'd definitely used protection!

'*Two* babies?'

She nodded, looking at him with concern. 'Identical twins. I had a scan this morning.'

He looked down at the ultrasound picture. He'd seen many over his years working as an obstetric surgeon, but to be passed pictures of *his* babies… Baby A. Baby B. He looked at them hard and

saw Rory's name at the top, her date of birth and
her NHS number. These were most definitely her
scans… And now they were his! The food in his
stomach churned and he couldn't look at his plate.

'I… I don't know what to say right now.'

A father—he was going to be a father. The
one thing that he was afraid of being, in case he
would be just like his own. All he'd heard growing up from his mother and his sisters was that
he was the spitting image of their father. He was
the only one of them who even had his father's
blood group! They were all O-positive, like their
mother, but he was A-negative, like his dad.

And for most of his life, from a teenager on-
wards, he had tried to do everything in his power
to be the opposite of that man who didn't deserve the title of father. He might as well have
just been a sperm donor. He'd never been home.
Never been to school events. Never supported
him in anything. He'd always been at work and,
if he was at home, no-one had been allowed to
bother him or disturb him because he *needed
his space*.

He'd been let down a lot by that man. It wasn't
just the appendicitis surgery he hadn't turned up
to; he hadn't shown up when Caleb had broken
his arm after falling from a tree. He hadn't come
to see him when he'd got the lead role of Dracula

in a school play. He hadn't turned up for birth-days, because he'd always been working. Christ-mases had been ruined by his absence. The only thing he had shown up for was to walk his daugh-ters down the aisle, and that had probably only been because he'd got to give them away and publicly prove that they were none of his con-cern any more.

Even that hadn't happened easily. He could remember hearing his mother shout at him that he'd better be there on the day or it would be the end of their own marriage. His sad had done his duty there, but at the receptions afterwards he'd seemed withdrawn and absent, even though he'd been right there!

Caleb could count on his hands the amount of times he'd actually sat down and had a proper conversation with his dad, and even then he was being generous in considering those events proper conversations. His father had often gone off on weird tangents and talked about something else entirely.

He had told himself he would not be like his own father and, to prevent that, his entire life plan had revolved around the idea that he would just never have kids himself. It would be one in the eye for his old man, not continuing on the Stride name, but tough.

And yet now Rory was telling him that she

was carrying his twins. There weren't enough words in his vocabulary to describe how he felt. Shocked, for sure. Afraid, no doubt. Guilty? Yes. Because already he was letting them down. Most committed fathers-to-be would be thrilled to hear that they were about to become dads but here he was, staring at the scan pictures and thinking of ways he could deny that all of this was happening!

'You're twelve weeks?'

'Yes.'

It tied in with that first time they'd done it in the hotel conference room. He believed her, too. They had to be his. Rory didn't screw around, he saw that—she wasn't that type of woman. She'd done nothing but work hard in the time that he'd known her and any down time she had was used for sleeping.

'I know it's a shock for you, so you need to take some time to wrap your head around it, like I did.'

'How long have you known?'

'Weeks.'

He looked at her. 'And you didn't say a word?' He didn't mean to raise his voice. It just happened.

'How could I?' She leaned in, blushing, her voice urgent again. 'I couldn't believe it myself, and what would have been the point in telling you if I'd only gone on to miscarry? Lots of first pregnancies fail and I was scared stiff!'

Of course. This wasn't just about what he felt but her too. 'You're scared?'

She nodded. 'But I'm keeping them, just so you know. If you don't want anything to do with these babies, then sure, eventually I'll understand, but my hope is that you will want to be involved.'

'Of course I'll be involved!' he said, raising his voice again then checking himself, remembering where they were. He didn't want to bring attention to them and he didn't like raising his voice to her either. It was just the shock. 'I can't not be,' he said, knowing it implicitly. Despite his fears about being a father, he had an obligation here, and he never shirked those. 'I'm just going to have to do my best.'

He couldn't let Rory down. Not her... Why *not her?* That puzzled him.

'That's all any of us can do. Think I know how to be a mother? We both know they don't send you home with a manual for these things.'

'Things?' he asked, trying to make the mood lighter, trying to distract himself from the fact that she somehow meant so much more to him than anyone else.

'You know what I mean.' She gave him a look then. A look so full of concern that it made him realise that they both felt exactly the same way: shocked and afraid. 'I think we just do what we can, as and when we can. And, somehow, we'll both just muddle through it.'

'Wow. Giving speeches like that, you'll have your own TED Talk in no time.' It was a flash of his old self. It was reassuring to know that he could still make a joke.

She reached across the table for his hand and took it in hers. He was surprised but he liked it very much. He knew no-one could see them back here, so he squeezed her fingers in reassurance. 'We'll find a way to do this.'

'We will.'

'Parenting. It can't be that hard, can it?' Though he knew all too well how quickly a person could screw it up. He knew the love of his mother, but he had not known the love of his father.

What might it feel like to be told by your dad that he was proud of you? Caleb was determined, somehow, that his own children, his twins, would *not* have to wonder how it felt. That he would be able to show them that he loved them, somehow.

He did not know how he would do that, and he feared his ability to do it, not having had a role model himself. But thousands of men became fathers every day and they managed it.

Maybe he wouldn't fumble the bag on this one.

Maybe, just maybe, he had the potential within him to be the greatest father in this world.

Now, that would be one in the eye for his dad, for sure.

CHAPTER EIGHT

As THEY WALKED back to the ward, Caleb stopped Rory just before they went through the secure double doors. 'You know, you and I—we should, um, get to know one another a little bit better. More than this, what we have right now.'

'I've been trying to do that, already.' Get to know one another a little bit better? For weeks now, Caleb had let her know that, though he wasn't a great catch, he would be happy to jump into bed with her at any moment. Whilst she appreciated the blatant fact that he found her sexually attractive, right now, pregnant with his twins, she wanted to know if he could see her as more than just a sexual being.

'I know and I reacted badly to that. But we should talk, spend time with one another, if we're going to be…' he looked around to make sure no-one was listening '…*co-parenting*. I think we ought to know who we're each dealing with a little bit more.'

He was right. She'd thought about that herself. And it wasn't as if he was asking her to be his girlfriend here. He'd nailed it with the word 'co-parenting'. They would parent these babies together, but that was *all* they would do. Except maybe be friends and colleagues. They would be in each other's life a lot! They just wouldn't be living together.

Would he still want to have sex with her, now that he knew? It would be interesting to see if he still flirted with her, or whether he considered her to be off-limits, now that she'd changed from being his hot sex buddy to the mother of his children.

'Okay. I agree. What do you suggest?'

'I was hoping that you might steer that ship. And that maybe, this time, I might be a bit more forthcoming.'

He smiled. He had a cute smile. She could look at it all day, to be honest. But he had to have more than that and a cute butt to do this with her. 'We should, I don't know, go out for a meal, or something? Somewhere we could talk that's not here.'

He nodded. 'Or…you could come to mine and I could cook. I'd like to cook for you for you again. Have I told you before about my world-famous cannoli?'

He had. He'd often bragged that he was just as skilled in the kitchen as he was in the bedroom. What else was he skilled at? Could he hang a roll of wallpaper? Fix a tap? Build a cot? Change a nappy? *I guess I'll find out one day.*

'Okay, dinner at yours. When?'

'When's good for you?'

'Tomorrow? I don't have as much nausea now, so… I could eat.'

'Perfect. Seven o'clock?'

She smiled. 'Seven o'clock.'

They made a pact to meet up and eat together at least twice a week for the next few weeks, as they got to know one another. To begin with, Rory felt nervous each time. What they were doing was stepping way beyond her usual tactic about knowing a guy. She'd had a one-night rule for a reason—she didn't want to have to get to know someone, because what if they let her down again? What if they humiliated her, the way Leo had? What if Caleb walked away and left her to deal with this on her own? And yet here she was, forced into a situation in which she *had* to get to know Caleb, no excuses.

It was scary stuff! *But,* she reasoned, *it's not like I'm getting into a romantic relationship again. It's not like this is going to end with me donning a white dress and walking up the aisle again, only to find it empty at the other end.*

Caleb seemed committed to the idea of co-parenting, to giving it his all, as much as he could,

promising that he *would not* let her down. But
so had Leo. He had put a ring on her finger and
promised to marry her. Promised to be by her side
until the end of their days and yet, when she'd
turned up to that church, he'd not been there.
He'd chickened out at the last moment. Some time
later, when they had met to talk, he'd said marriage wasn't for him—and that actually, when he
thought about it, marriage *to her* was not what
he wanted. That there had, in fact, been someone
else, someone *better* than her. Being abandoned
had been bad enough, but being abandoned and
finding out she'd already been replaced had been
another level. It had been a hard punch to the gut,
and in front of all her family, all her friends. Everyone from work knew about it and had watched
her try to recover her dignity and act as if it had
never happened.

What if Caleb said all the right things, promised her and the babies all the right things, but
then abandoned her when the babies arrived? It
could happen. And that would be even worse.
So this process of getting to know him was incredibly important. She was trying to see inside
his soul.

Yes, he was a great cook, he had a nice flat and
amazing bookshelves, filled with a wide range
of fiction and non-fiction, but what did that tell
her about him? His flat was neat and cared for.

Pictures of his mum, his sisters and their children abounded, so he was a family-oriented guy. But it was one thing to be a great son or a great brother. Being a father was a struggle for a lot of guys, and he'd told her right at the beginning that he didn't want to be one, that he had father issues—now these babies in her belly had forced them both into a corner.

And what happened to people forced into corners? They fought their way out.

'This looks great,' she said, lifting a lid from a pan to see what was cooking.

She was round at his again, eighteen weeks' pregnant and feeling much better. The glow promised to most pregnant women was an actual glow now, and not just a fine sheen of sweat from her nauseous stomach. People at work knew she was pregnant. They knew that Caleb was the father. It had started the gossip mill going, but they were riding that storm.

'It's white bean stew.'

'Stew?'

'It's good for you, and it has the added benefit of tasting amazing with the Irish potato bread I've made.'

'You're so domesticated. I like it.'

She'd quickly discovered his love for cooking. It was something he'd taken up during his time away at medical school, needing to find a relaxing, yet creative, outlet. It turned out that Caleb Stride, sex god extraordinaire and father of her babies-to-be, had actually been the resident cook and baker in his halls of residence, filling the building with aromas of fresh bread or apple pies, or knocking on doors to share muffins and slices of lemon tart.

The fact that he'd found time to do that around the masses of studying they'd had to get through amazed her. She had no doubt that Caleb must have been popular, especially with all the young women. But she didn't like to think about that. How many had come before her?

'You find the time for the things in life you love,' he said. 'Cooking, I mean,' he added awkwardly, as if his statement implied that, by cooking for *her*, he loved *her*.

They'd both stayed away from discussing them being in any kind of relationship, except a parenting one. They spent time together. They laughed, told stories, watched movies and bonded over books, music and food, but the big questions... They hadn't really tackled them yet, but Rory knew that needed to happen. She was almost halfway through this pregnancy.

'Oh!' Rory suddenly stood up straight and rubbed at her growing belly.

'Everything okay?'

'Yeah, I think I felt something.'

'Like a kick?'

She'd been aware of some weird swishy feelings, as if something was softly stroking the inside of her belly, but that was all. This was different—more...forceful. 'Maybe? I don't know.'

'Where was it?'

She reached for his hand and placed it on her bump where she'd felt the kick. They stood like that for a while, waiting, wondering, hoping, and were about to give up when it happened again.

A smile crept across Caleb's face. 'Oh my God.'

Rory laughed in shock. 'There's a real person inside me.'

'There's two.'

She looked at him and nodded, still in disbelief that her body was doing this.

'You've got another scan coming up soon, right?'

'Yes. The anomaly scan.'

'I'd like to attend that one, if that's okay?'

'Of course. Why wouldn't it be okay?'

He shrugged. 'I know I couldn't attend the first. You were going through some stuff on your own and I understand that. But I don't want to miss any more. I want to be there for everything.'

'Then you'll be there.'

He nodded and turned away to stir the stew.

She felt he had something else he wanted to say. 'What is it?'

'Nothing.'

'No, say it. If we're going to do this, we have to be able to talk to one another. To ask the difficult questions.'

'I don't want to be like my dad. I want to be there for everything. And the idea that we'll co-parent but live apart is doing my head in. Because there will be things that will happen when I'm not there: the first word, the first steps. I'll either be at work or here and, though I could be round at yours a lot, there will still be things that I'll miss. Moments that both parents should see, experience.'

'I know you don't want to be like your dad, but what are you suggesting? It's not like we can live together.'

'Why not?'

'What?' She couldn't believe that he was asking this. *Live together? Move in and actually live together?* 'But...we're not...going out or anything.'

'I didn't say anything about romance, I said living together. Lots of people live together. House mates. Lodgers. We could find a place and do that. That way, we're both there, but we still have our own independent lives.'

'Find a place?'

'Well, your place isn't big enough for all of us and neither is mine. We could rent a place together—move in. That way these babies get their mum and their dad in the same place and I won't feel like I'm missing out on my kids or have to make appointments to see them. Do you know how sad that would be if I had to do that?'

'I get it,' she said, understanding his concern. But moving in together? That was a big thing to decide. A huge life choice!

She'd already fought a bombardment of questions from her mum and family as to who this guy was, why they weren't together or getting married and how the co-parenting was going to work. How would she explain *this* suggestion? Would they think it a good thing, or just tell her she was making another huge mistake in renting or buying a property with a guy who wasn't committed to her, only to the babies? Her mum had already worried about him wanting to take them and go for custody. She'd even suggested she get him to sign something to say he wouldn't take her grandchildren away from her.

'Think about it,' he urged, bending down to open the oven and check on the potato bread.

She nodded. She would. But it was a huge commitment. The last time she'd tried to make a huge commitment with a guy, it had all gone terribly wrong and her life had been ruined. What if the same thing happened here? What if they ended up hating one another, or unable to speak to one another? Would the babies be affected too? Before, all she'd had to worry about was herself. The only person she'd had to pick up and shake down was herself. But this time there was more at stake. She had to think of her children too. What was best for them? And what was the least risky thing for her?

Could she trust him—truly? She had to trust him with the babies—he was their dad and he wanted to be part of their lives, for which she was grateful—but what if he let them all down? What if he couldn't be a good father, the way he feared? Would she be exposing them to possible emotional pain further down the line, when her children would one day blame *her* for putting her trust in a guy who had told her from the outset that he'd never wanted to be a father?

What if he was playing a role? What if this was just some sort of game to him, with which one day he would grow bored, the way Leo had grown bored with her and picked someone else? She saw it in plenty of fathers at the hospital. The babies in their partners' bellies were exciting, fun, and they had all these dreams and hopes. But then during the birth, watching those babies emerge, seeing a real-life person actually

get birthed and realising that they were responsible for it hit home. It scared them.

And some of them backed away completely.

Caleb was nervous sitting in the waiting room,
waiting with Rory to go in for the anomaly scan.
She was a little over twenty weeks now and this
would be the first time he would see them for
himself. He'd watched her grow bigger, had felt
them move and kick, and that was amazing. It
was different when it was his own. He'd watched
and coached so many women through labour and
delivery no matter how it happened, watched a
woman and a man transform right before his eyes
into a mother and father, a family.

But, now that it was happening to him, he
could understand even more all the worries, the
fears. The apprehension at holding them right, at
taking them in their arms for the first time, terrified that the world might somehow do them harm
the second they exited the hospital. Being an obstetric doctor, he'd always assumed that if he ever
became a father, which he'd strongly doubted, he
wouldn't be that worried at all. He'd been wrong.
And it made him question his own father even
more. Had he not felt the same thing? Had he not
wanted to protect them all?

Caleb had discovered that he was, if anything, worrying excessively, afraid that any mis-

step would somehow prove to the world that he wasn't good enough to look after them properly. And this anomaly scan—what if it showed something wrong with the babies, something genetic? What if there was something wrong with him at genetic level and he was a carrier of something and had somehow altered his children's lives even before they'd been born?

Being an obstetric doctor, he knew there was so much that could go wrong with identical twins. Twin-to-twin transfusion syndrome, for one. Then there was TAPS to worry about: twin anaemic polycythaemia sequence, in which one twin could be severely anaemic and the other polycythaemic, meaning it received too high a blood count. There could be amniotic fluid issues: too much or too little. What if their cords got entangled? Identical twins statistically had a higher risk of birth defects.

All these worries and more swirled around in his brain, knowing he was defenceless against them all, that he could do nothing about them. He couldn't protect them from any of it!

'Have you had any thoughts about what I said the other week?' he asked to distract himself from the vortex of worry sucking him down. 'About getting a place?'

She glanced at him. 'Erm… I've thought about it non-stop.'

'And? When are we moving in together? Living in sin? Having sex morning, noon and night?' He smiled.

She gave him a playful nudge. 'Is that what you think is going to happen?'

'It'd be fun, wouldn't it? You can't get any more pregnant, though I'd be happy to try.'

Rory smiled. 'It's a big decision.'

'So is bringing babies into the world and we're doing that together.'

'We had no choice in that.'

'True. What's worrying you about getting a place?'

'Who said I was worried?'

'Well, if you weren't worried, we'd be looking already.'

'I just don't want to make a mistake, Caleb.'

'Thanks.'

'No, you don't get to be like that. You're asking for a huge thing from me. Get a place together? Move in with you to raise these babies together? What happens when it all goes wrong? What happens if you meet someone else, or I do? And when one of us falls head over heels with someone else and wants to live with them—what then? People leave when that happens.'

'It's never been in my life plan to fall in love and get married,' he said.

'It was never in your plan to have children and

that's happening,' she replied, raising an eyebrow at him, just as her name was called.

They stood up and went into the small darkened room, where the technician introduced herself and Rory lay on the couch, exposing her abdomen to be scanned. She looked healthy, full...ripe. His babies were in there!

But what she'd just said to him was right. What if he did meet someone he couldn't stop himself falling in love with when he was living with Rory? How would another woman feel about him living with his baby's mother, but saying it was totally innocent? Clearly it hadn't been at one point! Would he move out? Would he put this *other* romantic relationship before his kids? Would he make the choice to make his kids take second place in his affections and promise that he'd still visit as often as he could, but would split his time between homes? His father had left one family and made another, and apparently had come back begging for a second chance after realising his mistake. Was he doomed to make a mistake too?

And what if *she* met someone? Someone who loved the babies and her and wanted to slide a ring on her finger and take care of them for the rest of their lives? Would she ask Caleb to move out? Would she just take the babies and go?

There were so many uncertainties and they re-

minded him that he needed to harden his heart,
to put up some barriers just in case, so that he'd
be prepared for any eventuality. Maybe moving
in together was a bad idea, in that case. Perhaps
they *shouldn't* get a place, and he should accept
the fact that he would just have to make appointments to be able to see his kids.

'This might feel a little cold,' the technician
said, squirting gel onto Rory's belly.

Then she moved the Doppler, he could see his
babies on the screen and it was the single most
glorious thing he had ever witnessed. His babies!
His twins! One was sucking its thumb! His heart
melted in that moment and all his fears disappeared for just a second as he sat and marvelled
at what he and Rory had created between them.
The measurements were good. Both babies were
doing well and, at the moment, there appeared to
be no sign of anything being wrong, which was
fantastic news!

Had his father marvelled at his wife's growing bump? Had he placed a hand on her belly
to feel the kicks? Had he cared? Would he have
connected with his children better, if he could
have seen them like this? Could have heard their
heartbeats and watched them slip and slide in
the womb?

'Well, everything looks good at the moment.
As these twins are sharing a sac and a placenta,

we will probably want you to come in weekly so we can keep an eye on them—check for cord entanglement and check their cerebral arteries. Don't be alarmed by it; it's all done for safety, so we can get ahead of any potential problems that may arrive.'

Rory nodded. This was because their twins were MCMA twins—monochorionic monoamniotic twins. They'd the same placenta, same sac.

'Would you like to know the sex?'

They'd not discussed that. Caleb glanced at Rory. 'I don't mind. You choose.'

'I think I'd like to know.'

The sonographer smiled and moved the wand around Rory's abdomen to show them what they were having.

'Twin girls!' he said, surprised. *Daughters*. Daughters were precious. They'd need protecting from this cruel world. He felt a wave of protectiveness wash over him, a wave of duty, care and love.

Rory hiccupped a laugh and that was when he realised she was crying. He passed her a tissue from a box conveniently on a table beside him. 'We'll have an earlier delivery, won't we?'

The technician nodded. 'Usually MCMA twins are delivered on or around thirty-two to thirty-three weeks. You'll be able to discuss this with your consultant.'

'He'll prescribe me steroids—for the babies' lungs to mature?' Rory asked.

'Yes, but again that's something you'll discuss with your consultant. You're under Mr Atwood-Green?'

'Yes.'

'He might also suggest daily foetal monitoring when you reach twenty-four to twenty-five weeks. Babies move all the time and we'll need to check for entanglement.'

'We could do that at our own hospital. We work at St Henry's and he consults there too. It's why we picked him.'

'Then I don't see why that would be a problem.' The technician smiled and passed them a few pictures from the scan.

'So, I'll be a caesarean,' Rory said as she got up into a sitting position.

Caleb nodded. It was the safest delivery for this rare type of twins.

'Thank you.'

They thanked the technician and left, clutching their pictures and feeling happy that the growth of both twins was fine. The risks of Downs was low and, because Rory had a nice long cervix, there was no risk of her going into premature labour.

'So, I've got a few more weeks of freedom, then daily checks for what—nine weeks? Then deliver?'

'Looks like it.'

Rory sighed. 'I knew this was complicated, but now it's just getting more so. What if something goes wrong?'

'I think it's natural to worry, but everything's fine right now. Let's keep that in our minds and carry on as normal. Let's only worry when there's something to worry about.'

She nodded. 'Identical twin girls. Daughters.' She shook her head and laughed. 'Can you believe it?'

He smiled, but as they got to the car, he looked at her over the roof of it. A sudden determination filled his soul. 'I have to be there for them. To protect them. To love them. To marvel in their every day. I don't want to have to make an appointment with you to see them. I know that makes it complicated, and what might happen if one of us meets someone else but, like I said, let's cross that bridge when, or even if, we come to it. We'll work it out then. Let's get a place. What do you say?'

Rory stared at him, biting her bottom lip as she thought. 'I don't want to make a mistake, Caleb.'

'Neither do I. But I do feel that living apart from my children would be a huge one. I can be there for them, we can share the care... I can help. I want to be hands-on. I *have to be* hands-on. I can't do this any other way.'

Rory nodded and got into the car.

* * *

'How many weeks are you?'

Rory's patient, Freya Young, was currently on a bed, strapped to the CTG machine and trying to distract herself from her own fear of giving birth by concentrating on someone else. 'Twenty-one,' she said.

'Halfway!' Freya said. 'Do you know what you're having?'

'Twin girls.'

'Twins? Oh, how exciting! Hard work, though, I'd imagine.'

'All babies are hard work,' Rory agreed with a smile as she checked the trace. The baby's movements had reduced somewhat, but the heart tracing was good, and Freya was contracting four in every ten minutes. They were monitoring the baby because Freya had developed gestational diabetes in the last few weeks of her pregnancy, and the baby was large, but had slowed down with its movements. Midwives usually suggested to expect to feel at least ten movements every couple of hours, but all babies were different, and it was important that each individual mother got used to her own baby's movements and noticed if anything changed.

Freya had noticed a drop in the last week and she'd been admitted for monitoring. Her labour had been induced, as her waters had broken with no sign of starting labour on her own, and there'd been some mild green staining in the water, indicating the baby had passed a stool in utero.

'And a worry. I don't know how I'm going to do this on my own.'

'You're not on your own, you've got me,' Freya's mum said, rubbing her daughter's shoulder.

'For this bit. But you live four hours away, Mum. You can't stay for ever. I'm going to be on my own for the majority of it.'

Rory's mum was close enough. Maylee was an hour away. She knew Caleb would want to be by her side for the caesarean and, now that she'd agreed to them getting a place, they would no doubt have to move in with one another soon and get used to living together. Would it be awkward? They hadn't slept together again since he'd found out about the pregnancy, despite the hormones flooding her system and making her hyper-aware of him and his proximity. Would they be able just to stick to co-parenting in their house? Or would they succumb to their desires, slip into each other's beds and make this even messier than it already was?

Since Caleb had suggested they move in, that they take such a big step, she'd noticed herself watching him. Every time he spoke to another woman at work—a midwife, a nurse—or every time he laughed with them or she saw them flirting with him, she felt a warning pang that this could all go so badly for the babies and her. She didn't want to feel jealous or worried. It wasn't as if he was her boyfriend or anything, and she had no right to be jealous, but she couldn't stop herself from noticing. He was an attractive man. He was bound to attract attention.

Caleb had said they'd discuss it later down the line if either of them met someone, but honestly, Rory couldn't imagine meeting someone else. It wasn't as if she was going to be out on the town, or clubbing. She'd either be at work, working or home, trying her hardest to raise two daughters! But Caleb might meet someone. He wouldn't get the maternity leave that she would, so he would be at work whilst she was at home and the hospital was filled with plenty of attractive young women who might flirt with him. And she knew, from her own experience, that he was a very sexual person.

What if, whilst she was at home changing dirty nappies, juggling bottles and laundry, not able to shower, Caleb was at work getting it on with a nurse in a linen cupboard? The thought disturbed her and the fact that she *was* disturbed disturbed her even more! She had no claim on him. It wasn't as if they were courting, going out or boyfriend and girlfriend.

Did she want him to be? Or were her hormones just playing games with her mind? Perhaps, if her brain wasn't sodden with oestrogen, then she wouldn't care about that at all! Yet at the moment her lizard brain was drunk and simply creating the idea that the father of her children was going to be her partner simply by them moving in together.

He'd already found them places to look at. Ever since she'd given him the nod after the scan, he'd scoured websites and noticeboards and found a lovely house, suitable for raising the twins, with vacant possession close to St Henry's, but far enough out that it was big enough. It overlooked a park filled with trees and beautiful walks by duck ponds for the days when they'd be out pushing the twins in a pram. They could move in on Saturday if they liked it. Caleb had done all the searching, all the phone calls and all the scouring of estate agents' websites. He'd even begun to help her pack and get things into boxes, ready.

Her sex god had turned out to be a perfect cook, an amazing doctor, a packer, a caring, considerate person and hugely attractive father-to-be. It was rather disarming and cute and annoying all at the same time. Part of her was waiting for him to falter, just so she could go, *Aha! I knew you wouldn't be good at everything!*

But maybe that said more about her than it did

him. She always expected things to go wrong. Her relationships always had. Caleb was only meant to have been a one-night stand who conveniently lived and worked in San Diego, except now they were having a family and would be moving in together and working at the same hospital.

Thank you, fate.

'I'll be here for the first week. Get you into a routine, before I leave.'

'Thanks, Mum.' Freya suddenly grimaced as another contraction hit and Rory watched the tracing.

This contraction was stronger than the others and it lasted longer too. It was a good sign that things were moving on with the labour. She wondered if she would miss this—not going through labour, but having a caesarean.

'You're doing great.'

'I'm glad you think so,' Freya breathed once the contraction was over. 'I still can't believe I got myself into this mess.'

'Well, there's no going back now,' her mum said, smiling and squeezing her hand.

Rory could hardly believe her life now, either. After Leo, she'd believed her chances of trusting someone enough to fall in love with them and create a family were slim to none. She'd always wanted that happy little family, though: a beautiful house somewhere with a gorgeous, loving husband who worshipped the ground she walked on and couldn't do enough for her. Cute little babies to raise. But Leo had ruined it all and she'd not only grieved the loss of him and their relationship but her entire future. She'd believed the rest of it would be spent alone and yet here she was, moving into a rental property with the father of her babies—just some guy she'd had a wild night with. And now they were dealing with the consequences of co-parenting—but not in a loving relationship. She'd be going to bed alone.

But what if that could be different? She liked Caleb very much. He was sexy, talented and clever. She admired him as a doctor and the way he'd stepped up for her. The attraction between them was there, clearly, and if they were together then wouldn't *that* negate the worry of him bonking a nurse in a linen cupboard, or of him meeting someone down the line and wanting to move out?

Would he even want that? He'd never wanted to be a father, but here he was dealing with it. Maybe she could be brave enough to try and trust him and let him be closer—suggest a romantic relationship.

Rory shook her head. No. That was ridiculous. This was her hormones speaking, not her.

'What do you think?' Caleb had brought Rory out to see an end-terrace three-bedroomed townhouse. It had been newly built in the last decade, so quite modern in its architecture with lots of clean lines, large windows to let in the light, and it was softly carpeted in an oatmeal colour throughout.

They stood in the room that, if they took it, would become the twins' nursery. The windows overlooked the park outside at a view of trees and wide expanses of grass, intersected with narrow pathways. There was a small pond to the left with ducks and what looked like a solitary goose.

It was within their budget, an easy commute to St Henry's and it fell into the catchment area of three great schools, if they stayed here. He'd tried to think of everything—for the present and for the future.

'It's nice,' Rory said, wandering around, one hand on her bump, the other trailing the windowsill. At five-and-a-half months' pregnant with twins, she looked full-term already.

'Nice enough for us to want to put down a deposit? Nice enough to want to christen every room?'

She bit her lip, not going for the retort to his joke.

'What is it?'

'It's too real, is what it is. All of this…moving in. I know we've talked about it, but actually doing it is scary.'

He walked over to her and laid his hand upon her arm. 'I know it is. It's scary for me too.'

'Then why are we both doing something so scary?'

'Because not doing so would be even worse. For both of us. I wouldn't be the father I need to be and you would be on your own.'

She nodded, her eyes welling with tears.

He pulled her into his arms then and just held her. 'Tell me. Tell me who hurt you.'

Rory pulled back to look up into his eyes. 'Who said someone hurt me?'

'The hospital grapevine. I've heard things, but I'd really like to hear your side.' He'd heard vague snippets that had reached his ears after Rory's pregnancy by him had been made public knowledge. Some people were happy for them. Some were surprised that Rory had ended up pregnant after she'd sworn to never be in another relationship. Of course he'd asked them why, and they'd simply said, *ask her about Leo*. She'd never mentioned a Leo. But, since hearing the guy's name, he'd wondered if that guy had anything to do with Rory developing her one-night-only rule.

'Of course. I should have known that you can't have a private life if you work in a hospital.' She sighed, pushing herself away from him, and wiped at her eyes. 'Can we sit?'

There was nowhere to sit. The place had va-

cant possession. But they went to the stairs and
sat down on those.

'I was engaged to Leo. I loved him and we were
getting married. Things seemed great between us.
I was happy and I thought he was too. Initially, he
seemed to be excited about planning the wedding,
but as time went on he stopped doing it and left it
all to me. Said that he was happy for me to make
all the decisions for my big day, and I thought it
was because he just wanted to make me happy
and let me have the wedding of my dreams. We
didn't see each other much. We were both working hard at the same time.'

'Did he work at the hospital?'

She nodded. 'Leo was a general surgeon. He
doesn't work at St Henry's now. What I didn't
know was that he had begun to see someone
else—a nurse who worked in a GP practice.
Apparently they met at some party that I didn't
go to, because I was working a shift, but like I
say, I didn't know this at the time. But he'd become more and more distant as the wedding got
closer, and I just put it down to wedding jitters,
you know? I asked him if everything was okay
and he kept saying he was fine, so what was I
supposed to have done differently?

'Anyway, on the day of the wedding, I was in
my dress. I had driven to the church and, when we
pulled up, the best man told me that Leo hadn't

arrived yet and to circle the block again. Traffic was heavy, so I didn't worry too much—I just thought he'd been caught up in it. But everyone else had made it—all our colleagues at work, our families, our friends… When I turned up again, the best man was looking cagey and that's when he told me to check my phone.'

She paused. 'I didn't have it on me, but my mum had brought it in her clutch bag, and we checked it and there was an email—an apology, to say he couldn't go through with it. He didn't have the guts to say it to my face.'

Caleb shook his head in disbelief. *An email? What a coward Leo was.*

'My mum had to go into the church and tell everyone the wedding was off. I sat in the wedding car, crying my eyes out, heartbroken, with everyone I knew coming out and looking at me with pity through the windows. When my mum made it back out, we drove home. Thank God I'd booked two weeks off for a honeymoon I'd never take, because I needed those two weeks to lick my wounds and hide from the world.'

'I'm so sorry you had to go through that. You deserved more than an email. You deserved a proper apology. A face-to-face apology and an explanation. Did you get one?'

'Eventually. We met for a coffee and he explained he'd met someone else. Someone who he

loved more than me. Told me that they were trying for a baby. That he could see marrying her
one day, and that he hoped I'd understand that
you can't help who you fall in love with or when.
That our time together was never meant to be.'

Caleb was in shock. If he ever came across
this Leo…

'And he was right. You can't help it. I'd fallen
in love with someone who was unreliable and not
committed to get through the tough times with
me. I'd fallen for someone who had humiliated
me in front of all my colleagues. He left, but I
stayed and fronted it out. Eventually, as these
things do, other more juicy gossip came along
one day, and my trauma got forgotten. Mostly,
anyway. And so, yeah, I made a vow to myself
that I would never fall in love again. Never get
close to anyone romantically again. That all I'd
ever have with someone was one night, because
one night couldn't humiliate me in front of everyone I knew.'

'Until you fall pregnant with twins,' he said,
smiling.

'Until I fell pregnant with twins.' She smiled
back, gesturing with her hands. 'I'm afraid that
this will go wrong. That you will abandon me for
someone else at some point. I mean, let's face it,
you're a handsome guy—sexy, clever, available.
I've seen the way the midwives look at you, the

nurses, the female doctors. Someone is going to come along to claim your heart at some point.'

'Well, I appreciate the compliments, but I really don't see that happening.'

'No? You never thought you'd be a father and yet here you are, wanting us to rent somewhere because it's in a good catchment area.'

Caleb laughed. 'Life has a way of surprising you when you least expect it.'

'And at the most inopportune moments—which supports my hesitation and argument. I can do this alone, Caleb. It'll be hard, but with the support of my family I'll be able to do it. I just don't want to be abandoned in the middle of it.'

'I will never abandon my children.'

She gave him a pained smile. 'And me?'

'You're their mother.'

'Still doesn't answer my question. What am I *to you*?'

Caleb hesitated. How to answer this most difficult of questions? Rory meant a great deal to him and she always would. And, yes, he had feelings for her; how could he not? He was attracted to her sexually. He always wanted to spend time with her. But could he say anything more than that? It wasn't as if they were madly in love! 'I'm…very fond of you,' he managed.

'Fond?' She said the word like it was something ridiculous.

He flushed, feeling bad, feeling awkward, not wanting to show a commitment that wasn't returned. Maybe he could turn the tables in this uncomfortable situation. 'Well, what am I to you?'

Rory looked at him then, intently, sharply. Her eyes were still glazed with tears. But she was looking at him as if she was gauging something, trying to decide something. And then suddenly she leaned in and pressed her lips to his.

Surprised, he hesitated.

But then he began to kiss her back.

When she'd come to view this house, Rory had not thought that she'd be putting her cards on the table and kissing Caleb to let him know that she wanted more from their relationship.

I mean, I'd not really known for sure myself!

Hadn't the worst already happened? She'd been jilted at her own wedding. It had been awful, but she'd survived it, and she'd survive him too if the worst happened, but why not take the chance on a little taste of happiness first? They already had attraction and they'd skipped a few steps to start a family with one another, so why not fill out the middle bit too?

So she kissed him. Because in that moment it seemed like the only way to respond to his question, and it was something she'd been dying to do for ages—kiss him passionately, without it leading to sex. To kiss him because she needed to. Wanted to. To feel his lips upon hers again and savour it. Because it seemed impossible to have two totally hot nights with someone, have her world sexually rocked and not think about it all the time. Not want more of the same—his hands, his lips, his everything!

When they broke apart, breathing heavily, she gazed into his eyes, uncertain, unsure. What would he say?

'Well…that was unexpected.'

'But good…right?' she asked.

He smiled. 'Yeah. Better than good.'

'Okay.'

'Okay. So…we're doing this?'

'We're doing this,' she agreed, hoping that he knew she meant more than just a sexual relationship. She wanted, needed, more from him.

'Putting down a deposit?'

'Yes, and…'

'Having a relationship?'

She smiled and nodded, her heart thumping madly with happiness in her chest. 'Yes.'

'Boyfriend and girlfriend, not just mum and dad?'

'Yes.' He said it, because she couldn't. She'd kissed him instead. It was exciting, nerve-wracking and absolutely terrifying! But Rory felt, in that moment, that it was the right thing to do. She wanted her kids to know their father and, more than anything, she wanted them to be raised in a loving home. Not just one of mutual respect. It had to be more than that. She wanted it all. She wanted the happy-ever-after. Didn't she deserve it? Didn't he?

'Then I guess we ought to phone the lettings agent.'

Rory nodded.

'And then I need to take you back to your place.'

'Oh?'

'Yeah.' He smiled. 'I need to make love to my girlfriend. Is that alright?' he asked, his voice all husky and breathy.

'I can't think of anything better.'

CHAPTER NINE

'WE NEED TO get you to Theatre immediately, there's a prolapsed cord,' Caleb said to the mother whose delivery he'd been overseeing. He had his gloved hand inside the woman, trying to hold the baby off the cord so that it didn't become compressed and starve the baby of oxygen. It was an emergency.

The mother nodded, crying, her face all red and blotchy.

It had already been a difficult pregnancy for Mandy Tennant. She'd suffered hyperemesis gravidarum at the beginning that had hospitalised her, so she could be rehydrated with IVs. She'd gone into premature labour at twenty-eight weeks and been hospitalised again, but they'd managed to stop her contractions and place a stitch in her cervix. Then she'd developed an itch all over her abdomen in the latter weeks of her pregnancy due to a condition called intrahepatic cholestasis, which was caused by a liver condition in the mother. It had been suggested to Mandy that she be induced, as delivery of the baby sorted the condition and reduced the risk of stillbirth, and now the poor woman had a prolapsed cord!

The team managed to take Mandy straight to Theatre, pushing her on the bed all the way round. It was difficult to not press on the cord, but he really needed to avoid touching it to avoid it going into vasospasm, and as such they had Mandy on her knees, face down, to elevate her rear end, which was covered with a thin blanket to protect her dignity as they raced her through the corridor towards Theatre.

In Theatre, he immediately asked Rory to administer tocolytic drugs to help reduce Mandy's contractions as the caesarean was prepped for. The cord was still pulsating, which was good.

'This needs to be a category two section, please,' he instructed the anaesthetist. This was because there'd been no obvious sign of foetal heart distress, and Mandy had not been fully dilated when the cord prolapsed, so there was time for a regional anaesthetic rather than a full general.

Once prepped, they put Mandy on her back, put up the curtain and Rory was already slicing into Mandy's abdomen and was at the womb within seconds of beginning. The baby came out easily, crying lustily—a baby boy—and finally Mandy's crying turned from tears of sadness and frustration to that of happiness. A successful outcome was all anyone wanted in this situation and, yet again, they had cheated the odds and got one.

Afterwards, as they both scrubbed out, they stood at the sinks and smiled at each other. 'We're a good team,' Caleb said.

'We don't do too badly, if I say so myself,' Rory agreed.

They worked perfectly together as a team. They matched each other's energies and wants in bed. She was great to talk to and hang out with and he was beginning to see a future with her—a happy one, if he didn't screw it up.

Had he unexpectedly got lucky? Was it true what they said that, when not looking for something or someone, that thing or that person would arrive in life? He'd not wanted to be a dad and now he was going to be one. He'd not wanted to settle down with anyone and yet he'd rented a place with someone and they were going to move in, in the next day or so. They'd moved their relationship onto the next level. They'd committed.

Life was strange and full of unexpected twists and turns. All he had to do to keep up his side of the bargain was be there. *Not* let her down. *Not* abandon her. *Not* let his babies down—his *daughters.* And if he remained present, if he remained aware, he really couldn't see how any of it could possibly go wrong. He was a good guy. He might look the spitting image of his father, but he would not become him. His father had actually tried to call him recently, but he'd ignored the call. He'd decided that he would make *him* wait for attention for once.

Rory and his girls would always come first. No matter what life chose to throw at them.

Caleb wouldn't let Rory lift a finger as they moved into their new place together. It was sweet, really, the way he was taking care of her, and she could see that he was going all out to make sure that she and his babies were kept safe.

The first thing he moved in was a recliner chair and he made her sit on it, put a packed-lunch box next to her alongside a latte and her favourite book and told her not to worry about anything.

At first, she felt guilty about sitting there as the moving guys and Caleb carried in boxes and furniture, going back and forth from the van outside and back into the property. But after a while she began to enjoy it, especially when Caleb got a little sweaty and stripped down to a tee-shirt and jeans and she could see his biceps bulging and his hair grow a little damp from his efforts.

'How are you doing?' he asked her once, about three-quarters of the way done.

'I'm doing fine. You?'

'Yeah, we're nearly finished. I need to unpack

the kitchen stuff, so do you fancy a takeaway tonight, or do you want to go out?'

'A takeaway sounds perfect. How about pizza?'

'Sold.' He kissed her, smiling afterwards as he gazed into her eyes, making her feel special. Then he returned to his work and she sat there, wondering how on earth she'd got so lucky ever since she'd risked everything and kissed him. She'd not known how he might respond, but somehow she'd got everything her little heart desired. They'd rushed back to her place and they had most definitely made love, rather than had frantic sex. And making love to Caleb was everything she had ever hoped it would be. It was different from straight sex. There was something tender about it, something treasured. They'd laughed. They'd smiled. They'd breathed, gasped and moaned... in a good way!

And since that day, since they'd declared their intention to one another, their relationship had shifted onto a different plane—something more devoted, something more open. Her friends at work were so happy for her, especially after the debacle that had been Leo. They wished her all the best in the world.

Maybe it was time for her to get her happy ending after all. She'd had her fair share of trauma, upset and being alone. Of feeling second best. Of feeling as if she was never quite enough and controlling every aspect of her life since, so that life didn't slip away from her and do its own thing. And now? She was allowing Caleb to take some of that control, and it felt good to let go of the reins and to relax a little. He was doing everything he could to show her that he wouldn't let her down, and it was helping. She didn't feel as tense as before—her main worries now were for the pregnancy, even if she did still find herself watching how the other female staff interacted with him and worrying over every little smile, look or casually placed hand upon arm. Theirs, not his.

That evening, she gorged as much as she could on a scrumptious ham and mushroom pizza that was oozing with cheese and laden with pineapple, green peppers, sweetcorn and jalapenos. It was delicious, and clearly her eyes were bigger than her stomach, which took some doing. Afterwards, she sat on the chair, licking the grease from her fingers, and gave a satisfied smile, only to find Caleb staring at her. She smiled self-consciously. 'What?'

'Nothing.' He smiled back, still eating his own triple-meat feast with spicy chilli beef.

'You think I should have eaten that with more decorum?'

'No, absolutely not!'

'I mean, it's probably going to give me horrendous acid reflux, but it was worth every bite.'

'I could tell.'

Rory laughed. 'You know, there's other parts of me that are still hungry...'

The pizza stopped halfway to his mouth. 'Really?'

'If you've got the energy after a long day hauling boxes and furniture?'

'I'm sure I could find it somewhere,' he said, putting down the pizza slice.

She held up her hands. 'Hold your horses, cowboy. This food needs to go down, first.'

He raised an eyebrow. 'I could do that too.'

Now it was her turn to look intrigued. 'Really?'

'Mmm-hmm.'

'Well, never let it be said that I don't give you what you want...' And she sighed contentedly as his fingers reached for her waistband.

At twenty-five weeks, Rory started her daily monitoring of the twins. She was called to the ultrasound department every day usually in the afternoon, as it was the best time for her, for the twins to be checked. Her fluid was measured, the cords were checked for entangling and the foetal growth-rate checked. There was a worry that, because they shared the same placenta, one twin might receive more blood or nutrition than the other, but so far her daily scanning had not shown any problems. Everything seemed to be going smoothly—the pregnancy, the babies, working with Caleb and living with him.

She'd thought worriedly that living and working together might be too much. That they'd be in each other's pockets excessively and that it might somehow cause friction in the relationship they were trying to build. Her past relationship with Leo had taught her to be on constant alert, always looking for signs of discontent. She'd felt Leo pulling away, but had excused it, blaming it on wedding pressures, not realising it might be something—or someone—else. So she felt that, even though she had to trust Caleb with her happiness, she should also make sure his dedication to her was one hundred percent at all times, because anything less meant that she could potentially lose him.

So when she entered Maternity that afternoon, looking to see if he was free to go to her screening with her, she was alarmed to see him leaning on the desk surrounded by three young, beautiful midwives, Morgan, Shana and Trina, who were all smiling at him and laughing at some story he was telling them.

The surge of jealousy she felt hit her like a wave, but she tried to tell herself that she was being ridiculous. He was committed to the babies and her. There was no reason he'd want to cheat on her with these gorgeous—slim—women. Was there? They were all gazing up at him happily, eyes gleaming, laughing coquettishly—one of them holding out the chocolate tin for him to pick from, as if sharing her own favourite. *I like this one. It's creamy...*

'Caleb?'

He turned and his face lit up even more. He didn't act guilty, so that was good, but then again he was a confident man, comfortable in his own skin, and no doubt comfortable being around women. 'Rory! Hey. Want a chocolate?'

The midwives all seemed to start at her approach, and returned to whatever they'd been doing, one of them giving her an appraising look over the desk. Did she harbour thoughts about Caleb's relationship with her? Because Rory was not going to let any slip of a thing ruin what she had.

'No thanks. I've got my scan in a minute, are you free to come with me?' She didn't mean her voice to sound tense. She just couldn't help it. The midwives had disturbed her.

'Sure.' He turned back to the others. 'You ladies can have me paged if anything urgent crops up whilst we're downstairs, right?'

They nodded and smiled at him, before gathering files and going about their jobs, dispersing because *she* was there now, when they'd gathered like a flock in Caleb's presence.

'They all seem to like you very much,' she observed as they headed to Ultrasound.

'They're a great bunch. A good team.'

'Uh-huh.'

He paused for a moment. 'Have I done something?'

'Not yet. As far as I know.' She hated sounding jealous and churlish, but she couldn't help it. Her body was flooded with hormones and sometimes it meant she thought and acted irrationally.

His hand steered her towards a linen room and he closed the door behind them and turned to look at her. 'What does that mean?'

She flushed, feeling awful, but also unable to stop herself. Her emotions surged, let loose. It didn't help that she was as big as a house and felt cumbersome, not as attractive as she used to, even though Caleb had made it perfectly clear that he found her just as appealing sexually as he had before she was pregnant. 'They all want you, you know! I can tell. I can see it in their eyes!'

'They're just being friendly.'

She scoffed. 'That's what every guy says.'

'Rory. Nothing is going on.'

She wanted to believe him, and she hated that she was being like this, but all the hormones were making her see things that weren't there. She sighed. 'I'm being stupid.'

'No, you're not.' He tipped her chin with his finger to make her look at him. 'What's wrong?'

She shook her head, but then thought of his words. There was a lot at stake and they had to be able to talk to one another. 'I just saw you there with all those midwives and it made me feel jealous.'

'Why?'

'Because they're all young and slim and beautiful and hanging off your every word and I'm…' She sighed. 'I'm not.'

'So you're saying only slim women are beautiful?'

'No! Of course not!'

'Rory…you're the most gorgeous creature I've ever seen in my life. I knew it the second we met. And now, now that I know you even more, now that you're filled with my babies and nourishing them, protecting them and fighting to give them a future with their father, you're even more beautiful. I find you irresistible—sexy, curvaceous. Those midwives are nice. But that's all they are— co-workers. Colleagues. And, if you can't trust me, then I don't know what we're doing—and we're going to have a problem.'

She wanted to believe him. She really did.

But history had taught her not to believe a man when he promised her everything.

'What have you done to yourself?' Caleb stared at their fellow obstetric surgeon, Mr Alex Michaels, as he came into the staff room that morning with his left arm in a plaster cast.

'Can you believe, a trampoline accident?' Alex said, wincing.

'Trampoline accident?' Caleb laughed in disbelief. He couldn't imagine it.

'Oh, don't mock, my friend. You've got all of this to come, when your little girls want their daddy to join them for some backflips.'

'You did a backflip?'

'I most certainly did. Well, I *tried*. I misjudged it and, even though we've got that protective netting around it, it was weathered, it split and I fell out of the side and landed on my arm. Broke my radius and ulna near my wrist, hence this fashion choice.' He raised his arm once again to indicate that his girls had signed his cast with their names, pink love hearts and a message that said, *we love you, daddy xxx*

'So, no operating?'

'Nope. You and Rory will have to carry the load for a little while, if that's okay. Thankfully, it's my left arm, so I can still consult and perform examinations, but I'm limited for a bit.'

'No worries. We all pull together here.'

'Thanks, mate. How is Rory faring?'

'Yeah, good. No problems with the twins as of yet.'

'That's great. I'm glad to hear it. That's the only issue with working in this job. When it's your turn for your partner to go through it, you know intimately of all the terrible things that can happen or go wrong.'

'I know. But we're trying to live in the moment. Enjoy it and not fret too much about what might happen.'

'Very wise. You probably haven't got much longer to go, have you? When's her c-section booked for?'

'When she's thirty-three weeks. She's twenty-six weeks now.'

'Just under a couple of months, then?'

'Yes.'

'You'll both do fine, mate. I have no doubts.'

'Thanks. I hope so too.'

Caleb called Rory that day and told her that when he got home he wanted to take her out for a meal. Said it was important that they still made time for each other and celebrated each other, rather than focus all of their energies on just being pregnant. 'Let's celebrate having moved in together. It's quite a milestone for the both of us.'

Was he going overboard, trying to show her that she was important after her jealous outburst the other day?

At home, she watched him carefully through the reflection in her vanity mirror as he'd slipped into a nice suit. When he went downstairs, she picked up his work clothes from the bed and sniffed them, searching for traces of perfume or lipstick. There was none, and she felt ridiculous. What was she doing? If she wasn't careful *she* would be the one to ruin this!

She tried to take her mind off it by doing her hair and make-up. It wasn't something she did often, and as she did it she wondered why she didn't try more often with her appearance, if it made her feel better like this.

As she eventually came downstairs, he stood at the bottom and watched her, a growing smile upon his face, and when she got to the bottom she did a twirl. 'What do you think?'

'I think every guy out there tonight who sees you is going to want to be with you.'

'If they like whales.'

'You're gorgeous.'

'You *have* to say that.'

'No. I *get* to say that,' he replied, kissing her on the lips. 'Come on. I've got us booked into a nice little Italian place down by the river.'

He wasn't kidding. Dino's was on the waterfront, with an outside dining area lit by lanterns and candles reflecting light onto the water. It wasn't cold, so they chose to eat outside. Caleb pulled out her seat for her and then sat opposite. 'Hungry?'

'As a horse.'

He smiled. 'Good. That's what I like to hear.'

'Italian's my favourite cuisine, I think.'

'Mine too.' He gave the waitress their drinks orders and, when their mocktails arrived, they toasted moving in. 'To our future happiness.'

'Future happiness,' she parroted, trying not to think about how the waitress's eyes had gleamed at Caleb.

The menu was filled with every delight imaginable and Rory wanted to order everything! But in the end she chose an arancini starter and a Catalan lobster main served with green beans and new potatoes. They chomped on sesame-seeded breadsticks as they waited for their food to arrive.

'I see Alex is out of action for a little while,' she said.

'Yeah. He's warned me about getting on trampolines. Apparently they account for as much as half of all A&E admissions for activity-related injuries in children.'

'But he's an adult.'

'Yeah, but he's admitted to me he could be classed as a big kid, so...' Caleb smiled.

'It's a lot of extra work for us to carry. Is the chief going to hire a locum surgeon for cover, just in case?'

'I asked and apparently we don't have the budget.'

'Oh. What about when I'm on maternity leave? That'll be two surgeons down.'

'I guess it means I'll get overtime, if necessary. And our consultant, Mr Atwood-Green, has said he'll fill in for any emergencies, if we're booked.'

'But what about your paternity leave? That'll be three of us away; they'll have to hire a locum.'

'I'm sure the department is aware. We've told them the date for your c-section and they know that neither of us will be there for at least two weeks and then I'll be back. Now, stop worrying about something you don't have to concern yourself about.'

But she couldn't help it. Her worries had grown as exponentially as her waistline.

Their starters arrived, delicious aromas filling her nostrils and making her set aside her previous thoughts. Caleb was right: it wasn't her concern. The hospital was not going to leave the department without an obstetric surgeon. 'These look amazing.'

The restaurant was piping gentle violin music through hidden speakers and the view of the river was beautiful with the Houses of Parliament in the distance. The London Eye reached high into the sky. The low hubbub of conversation at the tables around them was soothing and they were just finishing their starter when a man a few tables across suddenly got to his knee and brought out a ring box to propose to his date.

Rory gasped, waiting to see if she would say yes. She'd never had a romantic proposal from Leo. He'd not gone out of his way to ask her. They'd been living together for a while and they'd spoken about marriage, and one day, he'd said, 'I guess we ought to get engaged if we're going to do this properly.' They'd gone out together and sourced a ring. Leo hadn't wanted to spend too much on it. He'd said the money would be put to better use in planning the wedding, and she'd agreed, just so happy that they were getting engaged.

But, until she'd seen the man on his knee right now, she hadn't realised just how much she envied the woman sitting opposite him. She was getting it all: a romantic riverside proposal. Her loved one down on one knee, taking her out for a meal and surprising her. A ring that he'd chosen all by himself. The woman gasped and said yes, and everyone clapped as the two stood up and hugged each other before sitting down again. The woman kept looking at the ring on her finger in awe, shock and happiness. Rory hoped that these two would have a better wedding than the one that she'd nearly had.

'That made you happy,' Caleb said.

'Of course it did! A little romance brightens anyone's day.'

'It strikes me that maybe you've not had much romance in your life,' he observed.

'How do you work that out?'

'Well, for instance, the way we met. It was wonderful, don't get me wrong, but there was nothing romantic about it. You had a one-night rule, so you'd done that sort of thing before, which means that no other guy would have had the opportunity to date you. And your cowardly fiancé, Leo? I don't know him, but I reckon he wasn't the romantic type.'

'And you are?' she asked teasingly.

'Of course.' There was a small bud vase on their table, filled with a sprig of flowers, and he pulled one of the tea roses from it and presented it to her. 'A rose for my rose.'

She laughed. 'Smooth. What else have you got?'

'That's it. I'm out.' He smiled and sipped his drink. 'Apart from the fact that I arranged a romantic dinner date by the river. What about you? What moves do you have?'

'I guess I've never really thought about it. I suppose I always hoped it would just happen to me. That I would find the right person and somehow, during our relationship, I would be wooed and courted and made to feel special—and that I would do my best, in turn, to make the other person feel the same way.'

She sighed. 'And I want to make you feel special, Caleb, but let's face it—romance is probably going to take a back seat now. We're going to be parents soon—sleep-deprived, exhausted, wearing clothes that ought to have made it into the wash a week ago. I'm going to be wandering about the house in stained pyjamas and unwashed hair, probably smelling of baby vomit. We're not going to have time for romance until they're about eighteen years old, and by then we probably won't even bother. If we're still together.'

'What a bleak future you describe. Maybe you should stay away from writing any romantic stories.'

'I'm being a realist.' Reality worried her. Horrible things happened in relationships when the newness and excitement had worn off and she and Caleb had not got together the usual way.

'So am I. There's always time for romance. If it's important, you make the time.'

'And is it?' she pressed. 'Is it important to you?'

'With you? Absolutely.'

He wanted to be a man who would remain true to his word. It was a mantra he had always lived by—if he made a promise to someone, then he kept it, as he refused to be like his father, who had always been a man to go back on his word.

He remembered turning seventeen, getting his provisional licence and wanting to learn to drive, and he'd asked his dad if he would take him out driving and help him learn. His dad had vowed that he would find the time. He'd said he knew he'd let Caleb down before, but he would find an hour for that. He managed it twice. They'd clashed in personalities. His dad was an absolute stickler for the rules, yet hadn't made himself clear in his instructions to Caleb—so they'd argued, and his dad had just stopped teaching him. He'd had other stuff he needed to get done and he didn't have an hour every day to take his son out.

After weeks of this, Caleb had simply arranged to have lessons from a proper instructor, and his dad had never even said sorry. He'd clapped him on the back and said, 'Well done,' when Caleb had passed his test first time, but that had been it, and it hadn't been enough. His dad had never been enough and Caleb refused to be like him.

So the next night he presented Rory with a bunch of beautiful red roses when he got home from work. He cooked her favourite meal and took care of the washing up, before running her a nice warm bath, filling the bathroom with candles and piping soft piano music through a speaker. He massaged her feet when she needed. He rubbed her back when she needed. He popped out to get antacids when she got heartburn and always made sure that the house had a nice supply of ice-cream.

At work, whenever he caught her on a break in the staff room, he made sure she ate and had a drink, and he'd raise her feet up onto cushions, because he knew how much she hated her ankles swelling towards the end of the day. In Theatre, he helped her out and kept her amused when the twins began jamming their little feet under her ribcage, making her uncomfortable. He made time for her. He made her feel important. And he began to realise just how much he enjoyed doing so.

Maybe he wasn't like his father after all. Maybe all that fear and worry about turning out like his old man had been baseless. His life could have been completely different. And yes, of course it was easy to be thoughtful now; it was just the two of them. Would he be different when the twins were here and he was juggling sleepless nights and long days at work? That was where his fear lay, so he was probably trying to prove himself too much now, whilst he could. Especially since Rory seemed to have worries that it was all going to go wrong. He wouldn't let it.

'Here you go—strawberry milkshake, extra-thick.' He passed Rory a thick cup that he'd picked up from the milkshake bar down the street. 'You need it before you go into Theatre.'

'Oh. Thanks.' She wrapped her lips around the straw and sucked up the milkshake, moaning in delight as the first sip touched her tastebuds, delighting them.

'You've got a D&C?'

She nodded. 'Yes. Incomplete delivery of the placenta, so I'm going in to remove it.'

'Need help?'

Rory frowned and sighed. 'Don't you have your own patients?'

'I do. But none are emergent. I could help you.'

'I appreciate that, and I appreciate you taking care of me, but I am capable of completing my own surgeries, you know. I'm pregnant, not ill.'

'I like taking care of you.'

'I know, but… I'm okay. You don't need to do everything. I know I've been a lot, and I've been a bit down, but honestly, I'm trying to hold onto my identity before I become Mum—and that means being a surgeon.'

Was she telling him he was being *too much*? Maybe he was over-compensating, but he couldn't help it. He was so afraid of being at the other end of the spectrum.

'Okay.' He wasn't sure exactly how he'd feel about backing off, but maybe this wasn't about him. Maybe this was an issue *she* had. Her jealousies had increased tenfold since she'd got bigger. From what he'd heard about her relationship with Leo, he'd always been distant, and perhaps she wasn't used to so much attention.

'You should finish this off,' she said, standing and passing him the milkshake. 'I've got to go.'

He took it from her and watched her go, rubbing at the small of her back as she disappeared through the doorway.

Were they going to be okay?

He hoped so.

'Patient's asleep?' Rory asked, before she made a start. Caroline Carr lay on the bed in Theatre, draped in blue, her legs in stirrups. She'd given birth vaginally to a baby boy a few hours ago, and initially the midwives had believed her placenta to be complete. But in the post-natal ward Caroline had begun to bleed more profusely than expected, her womb wasn't fully contracting down the way it ought to and a quick scan had detected a piece of placenta left behind. Without it being removed, Caroline would continue to lose blood and possibly develop an infection.

'Away with the fairies and holding steady with her blood pressure,' Gavin, the anaesthetist, answered.

'Okay, I'm going to make a start.'

Rory loved Theatre. Sometimes, when she concentrated hard and the babies in her belly slept, she could sometimes forget that she was pregnant. But not today. Today, the babies were kicking hard and making her feel uncomfortable, and her lower back was beginning to protest at the extra weight and strain being placed upon it. *Only a few more weeks to go*, she told herself.

She began to dilate the patient's cervix using rods. She felt a little annoyed with herself, having spoken sharply to Caleb in the break room before surgery. He was only being nice, but she really didn't know how to deal with his constant attention. She ought to love it, she knew, but him doing so much… He'd brought her a huge bunch of roses the other day. The only time she'd been bought flowers before was when Leo had done something wrong and he'd felt guilty, so to her bouquets had a bad association. Flowers meant an apology. Flowers meant that the guy felt guilty about something.

Caleb was being *so* attentive! She hated herself for her jealousy getting out of control lately… She wasn't the usually sane Rory she knew, and it was because she was losing control of everything. Her feelings for Caleb were running away with her and she didn't like that. Her jealousy was making her snappy with him, and all because of her hormones. She had wanted to regain some control, to show that she was still independent and in charge. She needed that badly.

'Curette, please.'

Rory knew she would have to ask him to treat her normally. She wasn't fragile. She wasn't precious. She wasn't helpless. She might look like a beached whale, but she wasn't one, and she didn't actually need him to help her back into the water. Maybe if she got him to back off, she would feel better. But if she pushed him too far away…

'Here it is.' The piece of placenta that came out was actually tiny, but it was enough to have caused a problem. She checked the rest of the uterus and, when she was satisfied, she pulled off her gown and gloves and gave orders to the nurses to take Caroline through to recovery and monitor her.

As she scrubbed out, she felt a tightening across her abdomen that caused her to stop moving and just breathe. An early Braxton Hicks. She wasn't even thirty weeks yet, but her womb was the size of a full-term pregnancy already, so it was doing what came naturally. She rubbed her hand over her belly until it softened again and checked her watch. She knew to keep an eye out for any more and she would mention it at her

daily scan that afternoon. Maybe she'd tell Caleb
she could go by herself. He didn't have to attend
every single one.

CHAPTER TEN

'So, you're twenty-seven weeks and four days?' asked Barb, the ultrasound technician, whom Rory had got to know quite well.

'Yes, though I look and feel full-term. I think I had a Braxton Hicks earlier,' Rory said, lowering herself awkwardly onto the examination couch, lifting up her top and lowering her trousers waistband.

'Not surprising. This can often happen earlier in multiple pregnancies, though I guess I don't need to tell you two that.'

'No,' Caleb agreed.

She'd not managed to persuade him to let her come alone. In fact, he'd looked slightly alarmed when she'd suggested it.

'What do you mean, I don't need to come? Of course I do!'

'It'll just be like yesterday's. And the day before. And the day before that! It takes five minutes—what's the point in both of us leaving the department?'

'The point is that I get to be with you. The point is that I am there for my daughters.'

'I know you're here for us, Caleb. You don't have to prove it.'

'Yes, I do.'

She'd known she was not going to win this one so she'd backed down. She'd walked down with him to Ultrasound, giving the air that she was simply amusing his weird foible to be there. Secretly, however, she liked having someone to depend on, but she just wasn't used to it. She'd never known anything like the intensity of his devotion before. And, though it should have made her feel more secure, it was having the opposite effect.

As Barb ran the scanner over the twins, Rory lay there, marvelling as she always did at seeing her babies on screen. The daily scans were a comfort and she knew she was lucky to have them. Most women got scanned a couple of times during pregnancy and that was it.

'You're frowning, Barb. What is it?' Caleb asked.

Was she frowning? Rory had been staring at the screen but, now she looked at the technician, she felt her heart rate accelerate. 'Is something wrong?'

'We'd expect to see the babies grow by a few grams every day. I noted yesterday that Baby B had not gained weight like Baby A, and today's measurements confirm that baby B's weight has remained stagnant.'

'You think it's TTTS?' She meant Twin-to-Twin Transfusion Syndrome, in which one baby got more blood flow and more nutrients than the second twin. Most people assumed that that meant the bigger twin would somehow be stronger, but that wasn't always the case. Sometimes too much caused problems, too. 'Why didn't you say something yesterday?'

'Because I wasn't sure, and there was no point in worrying you unnecessarily, but today I can see it and I don't think it's an anomaly.'

Rory felt as if she might cry, but then she felt Caleb's hand grip her own, she turned to look to him for support and felt awful that she'd made him try to stay away. Imagine if she had been successful in making him back off and then this had happened when he'd not been there! He'd have felt terrible, and she would have been responsible for it. 'Caleb?'

'It's okay,' he said. 'They can monitor it, now they've noticed it, and we get daily scans, remember? How are the cords looking?' he asked Barb.

'Good. But do you see here—the blood vessels in Baby A's cord? They're larger than Baby B's—by millimetres, but they're larger.'

Caleb nodded. 'Is Twin B showing any decreased urinary output?'

Barb moved the transducer. 'Bladder looks full. All good for now.'

'So Baby B is the donor twin and Baby A the recipient,' Rory said. 'What can I do? Do I need laser therapy?' Laser therapy would allow a doctor to insert a fetoscope, a small camera, into the placenta under anaesthetic, and the identified blood vessels would be sealed with a laser. Mostly it worked, but sometimes the condition could return.

'I'll get the doctor to check the scans and confirm whether you need that, but for now we'll continue with the daily monitoring. You're booked in for an early delivery, so let's hope that the twins don't develop too diverse a weight differentiation.'

Rory did not feel reassured. She'd known this was a risk from the very beginning when she'd discovered she had morochorionic moroamniotic twins, but everything had been going so well, and she'd begun to believe that everything would be alright. Now the worst was beginning to happen, as she'd suspected it would.

Caleb helped her back up into a sitting position. 'I'll call Mr Atwood-Green. Can you send a copy of the scan to him for me, please?' he asked Barb.

'Sure thing. I'll send it to him straight away and ask him to give you a call once he's reviewed it.'

'Thank you.'

Rory's legs felt shaky when she got up off the examining bed. And she felt sick, too. She should have known that this wouldn't go right! Nothing ever went straightforward in her life and she should have expected this to happen. But she'd allowed herself to be hopeful, to assume that this time, everything would be okay.

It felt as though her world was on a knife-edge.

Caleb stood staring at the CTG tracing of his patient and tried to put the last few hours out of his mind. He'd spoken to Mr Atwood-Green and, after viewing the ultrasound, he had confirmed that nothing needed to be done just yet. He acknowledged that, though it was upsetting for Rory and Caleb to have been notified of the early signs of TTTS, there was no need to panic. It was early. It might not even fully develop into a surgical situation. They would continue to monitor Rory carefully and, as she was having daily scans to check for cord entanglement, then this could easily be done. If it looked as if Baby A, the recipient twin was getting too much of the blood supply, and it looked as if Baby B looked was suffering from that, then they would do something about it before it became a problem.

'But Rory is due for a c-section in just over a month. We might not need to do anything,' the consultant had said.

Caleb knew he was right. Not all TTTS patients developed an issue that needed surgery. Most cases remained mild but, like birth, it was only the horror stories he seemed to hear or remember. So, as he stood monitoring the trace of his new patient, he tried not to think about all of the TTTS patients whom he had seen himself, how many surgical interventions there had been, or how many times the situation had turned into a tragedy. Admittedly, it was a low number, but it did happen, and that scared him. And now he knew for sure exactly how those other parents had felt when they'd pleaded with him to tell them that everything would be alright.

'We're going to keep you on the CTG for a bit longer, Traci. Baby's having one or two decels and I want to keep an eye on them, okay?'

'Is the baby alright?'

He smiled. 'Yes. He's just letting us know that, on occasion, the contractions aren't agreeing with him.'

Traci nodded, but he could see the fear on her face and on that of her husband. This was an IVF baby, a baby who had been wanted for so long, after many years of fruitless treatments and four miscarriages. This was the only pregnancy Traci had managed to carry to term, and he understood her fear of something going wrong at the last hurdle.

Did that fear ever go away? His own mum had told him once that being a parent was the most joyous, yet also the single most terrifying, experience she had ever gone through.

'The amount of times I've had to sit by your bed…fevers, the flu, appendicitis…that time you broke a bone and had to have surgery. You'll never understand what it feels like to get a phone call that your child is in A&E until you're a parent yourself.'

And he thought he'd never have to experience that fear. He had considered himself superior in the knowledge that he wouldn't, because he'd thought he would never have kids. And now he understood. His twin girls weren't even here yet and he was terrified.

But at least he'd been there, holding Rory's hand during the scan. She'd tried to tell him he could stay away, that she could manage on her own, but he'd been persistent and had still gone. Now he was so glad that he had, even though the news had been scary. How would she have felt to have received that news today on her own? She would have remembered it for ever—the day that he had not been there. And, worse than that, one day they would have told their children the story and they would have known too.

He never wanted his kids to think that he had not been there and, even if it killed him to do so, he would make sure he was there for *everything*. He couldn't help but think of his own father in that moment. The man had kept trying to call him and Caleb had ignored his texts, asking him to call him back. Even his mum had said that his dad needed to talk to him. But it was too late for all of that. His dad had had his chance to be a real father; Caleb was not going to let him screw up being a grandfather too. If Callum Stride thought for even one minute that he could suddenly put everything right, then he was wrong, and Caleb would not let his father fill his daughters' lives with disappointment after disappointment.

'I know it's easier said than done, but try not to worry. We have you and the baby on a monitor. Morgan here is a brilliant midwife, and she'll keep an eye on the CTG, and any changes, she's going to let me know. Hopefully, you won't see me again.'

'Don't take this the wrong way, doc, but I hope to never see you again.'

Caleb smiled. He understood. 'Don't take this the wrong way, but I hope to never see you again either. At least, not until after you've safely delivered this one, okay?'

They nodded.

'Got a name picked out?'

'Not yet. We wanted to see what he looked like first.'

'Caleb's a good name,' he said with a smile, then left the room, knowing that Morgan would contact him, or the next doctor on call if he had already gone home for the day.

Rory had already gone home. He'd told her to. She'd been a bit of an emotional mess after the scan and he just wanted her at home, relaxing. It was the best thing after a shock and he knew it would make him feel better to know that she was at home taking care of herself. He'd be there himself in an hour or two and he couldn't wait. He just wanted to hold her close, smell her hair and tell her that everything was going to be okay. Tell her that he would protect her and them, and he wouldn't let anything bad happen to them. It would break his heart if anything did.

He slowed to a stop in the corridor as he realised what he'd just admitted to himself.

It would break his heart. Which meant…

I love her. I love Rory.

He'd never admitted it to himself before. But, now that he realised it, he wanted to tell her! Wanted to tell the world! But…what if she didn't yet feel the same way? He didn't want to pressure her into saying it just because *he* had.

Maybe he would keep it to himself for just a little longer? Maybe now was not the right time to make declarations whilst she was riddled with anxiety and worry for their babies?

So he told himself he would hold the information deep inside for a little while—maybe wait until the babies were here—and then tell her?

Yes. That seems like it's the right thing to do.

CHAPTER ELEVEN

'SO NOW YOU'RE how many weeks?' asked the sonographer.

'Nearly twenty-nine.'

The sonographer nodded as she gazed at the screen, checking the cord as always, and measuring the twins. 'Well, you'll be pleased to know you're holding steady. Baby A is bigger, but Baby B has put on two grams in the last couple of days. Not as much as twin A, but she's growing.'

'So we can carry on as normal still?'

She nodded. 'Yes. You've seen Mr Atwood-Green?'

'Yesterday. He scanned me too; said he was happy and we didn't need surgical intervention yet.'

'That's good, Rory. That's really good.'

'Thanks.' The daily scanning had become a lifeline for Rory. She worried constantly about the twins and it was only the scans that reassured her that everything was alright. Every time the twins moved or kicked, she worried about cord entanglement. With every headache she developed, she worried about pre-eclampsia. Every time some-one told her she looked huge, bigger than the day before, she worried that Twin A was suddenly sucking up all the bloodstream and Twin B was being starved. She couldn't help it.

Caleb helped her into a sitting position as she wiped off the gel from her belly. 'Not long to go. A few more weeks. I think we can do this,' he said.

It was easy for him to say! He wasn't the one who felt like a ticking time bomb. Now she could fully understand the fear her patients felt. She'd thought she understood. She could empathise with them, but she had never *truly* known. But she did now. And she knew that Caleb was try-ing his best to reassure her, but he was still an outsider, looking in. It didn't matter how many times he rubbed her feet, brought her drinks or cooked her food—none of that could make up for the fact that she felt everything could go wrong in a mere moment and they might not know about it until the next scan.

And she'd seen the way the sonographer had looked at Caleb when they'd entered the room. They'd not met her before, as she was new, and she'd blushed. Rory had seen it with her own eyes!

She felt so alone, even though in reality she

knew that she wasn't. Caleb was there, and her mum was there phoning her every night, but still she felt alone, cumbersome and unattractive. Despite all her knowledge, despite all her skills, she could do nothing about what was going on inside her own body, and this lack of agency, after being in control of every aspect of her life for so long, was driving her insane!

What if she went through all of this and it still went wrong? What would happen to her then, to the babies, to her relationship with Caleb? *Because, let's face it, we only got together because of them.* If she lost them, how long would it be before he walked out of her life too?

'You're very quiet,' he said as they walked back to the maternity floor.

'I've got a lot on my mind,' she said, more snippily than she would have liked.

'I know what you mean.'

'Do you?' She stopped to turn and look at him, her anger and frustration at the situation coming out, aimed at him because he was closest and she had no-one else she could vent to. 'Do you actually? Because I don't see your body being the one screwing up a pregnancy and putting our children's lives at stake.'

She felt tears prick her eyes and she began to storm off. She'd not wanted to get angry, but it just happened. She was fed up with everyone's fake sympathy, pity and empathy. It wasn't real! They were just glad it wasn't them, and the only way to deal with her was to pretend that they understood.

'Rory!'

He caught up with her easily. Of course he did. He still looked as athletic and as fit as the day she'd met him, but she had grown to the size of a mountain.

'Just leave me alone, Caleb!'

'No! Stop. Rory, will you just stop for a minute?' He stood in front of her, blocking her way past him.

She shook her head, but she couldn't look at him.

'Look, I don't know what's happening right now, but if you're trying to provoke a fight then you're not going to get one. You can't push me away. You can't tell me that I don't understand. I know I'm not carrying those babies, but I would if it would help you. If it would make this easier. But there isn't anything to make this easy! The situation we're in, I get it—it sucks. I know it sucks. You think I want this? You think I want to see you like this, worrying all the time, crying in the shower? Don't think I haven't heard you.'

She flinched at that. She'd not realised that he knew.

'You have every right to be angry at the world

for this situation we're in, but you don't have a right to be angry at *me*. I'm *not* going to abandon you.'

'But you could. You could walk away. At any moment, if you wanted.'

'I don't want.'

She stared at him.

'You hear me? I don't want to walk away. I will *never* walk away. I'm not Leo!'

Her tears began to fall freely then, silently, hotly, fiercely. Was this where her anger came from—her fear? She feared losing the babies, she feared losing him. She feared being left alone again. She didn't want to have to go through that again. 'I know you're not.'

'Do you? I'm in this—for ever. Do you hear me? For ever,' he said, so softly. And he reached up and wiped away her salty tears, before pulling her into his arms.

She could feel the babies moving and kicking. They always did when she was in a place of high emotion. She wondered if he could feel them kicking, too.

'They hate it when we fight,' he whispered.

'Yeah.'

'So let's not do that.' And he kissed the top of her head.

Caleb was just coming out of Theatre the next day when he got bleeped to contact Mr Atwood-

Green. His first panicked thought was that it was about Rory. He knew she was on shift with him today, but as he'd been in Theatre so long he wasn't sure where she was. On the ward? Still in her clinic?

He went to the nearest desk and asked the staff where she was, only to see her emerge from a ward before he'd got to the end of his question. She was smiling, happy, sliding her pen into her scrubs pocket, before looking up at him. She frowned then at the worry on his face. 'You okay?'

'Mr Atwood-Green wants to see me. I thought it was about you.'

'Nope. Not as far as I know. It's probably for a case he wants to hand over or something.'

'It's the *or something* I'm worried about.'

'Want me to come with? I'm free at the moment, though I am closely monitoring a patient. If I stay on the floor, it should be fine if I get called in to deliver her.'

He nodded and they headed off to their consultant's office at the end of the corridor. Caleb rapped his knuckles against the wood door.

'Come in!'

He pushed the door open and saw James Atwood-Green behind his desk. Opposite him sat a young woman, about six months' pregnant, her face pale and tear-stained, and beside her was a man, also pale, holding the woman's hand.

James spotted Rory behind him. 'It's alright Ms Dotson, I've called in Mr Stride for this patient.'

'Oh, okay. I'll leave you to it.' Rory smiled and slipped away, closing the office door behind her.

'Mr Stride, this is Jennifer Boulter and her husband Hugo. Jennifer, Hugo, Mr Stride.' James indicated he ought to take a seat. 'I've asked you in here because I would like your assistance on this case.'

'Okay.'

'Jennifer is a primagravida mother, currently twenty-five weeks' pregnant with twins after an IUI procedure.'

Caleb nodded, knowing primagravida meant a first-time mother. Intrauterine insemination was when specially prepared sperm was placed directly in the uterus in the hope that the sperm located an egg in the fallopian tube to inseminate.

'She recently has discovered that she has an aggressive form of breast cancer that is oestrogen receptive and has been advised by her oncologist to start treatment straight away. Now, obviously this is a very distressing and confusing time for Jennifer and Hugo, and they are here to discuss an early delivery rather than termination.'

Caleb sympathised. What a terrible situation to find themselves in! 'Have we had a recent scan?'

'I've sent the details of the most recent scan to

your email, but basically the twins are non-identical, there's been no complications with the pregnancy, apart from some morning sickness which has now abated and no blood pressure problems. Twin A is measuring at twenty-four weeks and three days and Twin B is slightly larger at twenty-four weeks and five days.'

Ah. 'Okay, well, first let me say I'm extremely sorry to hear of your situation. No-one would want to find themselves facing what you are going through, but we are, so we need to discuss the best things for you, Jennifer, as well as the best things for your family as a whole. Has Mr Atwood-Green discussed the risks of an early delivery with you?'

Jennifer shook her head. 'Not yet. He wanted to bring you in first—he mentioned that you specialise in delivering early babies.'

Caleb glanced at James. 'Believe me, I would prefer not to, but I have had a lot of success in that area. The problem we have is that your twins are measuring at twenty-four weeks, which we class as extremely pre-term. It's four months early and that means that the babies are not as developed as we would like. When I say that, I mean the babies' organs in particular—their brain, their lungs, their heart—are very immature and not yet ready for the outside world. If we were to deliver them at this gestation, they could be, or may become, very sick; they'll most definitely need to stay in the NICU and have oxygen assistance.'

'But it's doable? Babies can survive at twenty-four weeks?' Hugo asked.

'There's an eighty percent survival rate,' Caleb confirmed.

Jennifer smiled. 'That's good, isn't it?'

'Yes, but that also means that one in five babies won't make it. You need to look at the stats that way, as well as positively, and try to prepare yourself for that eventuality if we go down this road.'

'But that's it?' Hugo asked. 'A ventilator?'

'They'll need round-the-clock care. They're at risk of many future complications...' Caleb explained what these were. It was a long list, but important for the parents to know so they could feel prepared.

'How many babies have gone on to have issues, in your experience?' Jennifer asked.

He thought for a moment. 'I'd need to check my figures, but nationally the average is about two in every ten babies delivered early will suffer from a mild disability.'

'Those are national statistics. How many in *your* experience?' Hugo pressed.

'About five in ten.'

'No matter what happens, we'll manage, Jen!' Hugo said, squeezing his partner's hand.

'It can be a difficult road, full of twists and

turns, and remember you're also going to be going through treatment, I assume. It's a lot of stress to handle, doing that and also visiting your baby in NICU.'

'I think I can do it,' Jennifer said. 'I can't lose these babies. I've already fought so hard to have them. Do you know how long we tried to get pregnant?'

Caleb shook his head.

'Four years. Four years of hoping every single month. Four years of monthly disappointments. Four years of trying not to be insanely jealous when all my friends seemed to get pregnant and start families at the drop of a hat! Four years of holding *their* babies in my arms and trying not to cry inside because I wasn't holding *my own*. Are you a father?'

Caleb didn't usually like to talk about anything personal with his patients, but in this instance he replied, 'I'm about to be.'

'You probably fell pregnant without trying, huh? It was probably easy for you and now you're about to be a dad without any worries in the world. Life's easy for some. Not for others.'

He was about to put her straight, but he glanced at James quickly, then looked away. James knew, but this wasn't the time to talk about himself. They were here for Jennifer and Hugo. 'When does your oncologist want to start treatment?'

'As soon as possible.'

'I'm sure Mr Atwood-Green would agree with me that the more time we can give your babies in the womb, where they belong, is the best thing for them all round. Even if it's just for a couple of more weeks…maybe get the babies measuring at twenty-six weeks. But we'll need to discuss this with your oncologist; what's their name?'

'Dr Waller.'

'Like Mr Stride says, we'll consult with your other doctors and come up with a plan for your treatment. We have space in our NICU, so that's not an issue, but I'd like to admit you sooner, rather than later, Jennifer, if that's okay with you? That way we have you here and we can keep monitoring you if we're able to keep you pregnant for another week or more. But, if we need to deliver asap, then you're here and there are no delays.'

'But I can go home? Pack, sort out some family arrangements?' Jennifer asked.

'Of course. But once we've spoken to your oncology team we really ought to admit you.'

Caleb excused himself from the meeting, left James to it and went to write up his notes from the surgery he'd performed before meeting Jennifer and Hugo. He really felt for them. What they had to be going through… Jennifer would no doubt want to be there in the future for her babies, but what if she wasn't and it was only Hugo left? Caleb couldn't imagine being in that situation. Losing Rory would be a terrifying prospect. Left alone to raise his twin girls…?

Once he'd written his notes, he grabbed the phone, dialled nine for an outside line and called his grandfather. He'd made a decision. When the babies were here, he wanted to give Rory something special—a gift to show her how much she meant to him. He'd heard the nurses call it a 'push present'. And, if he was going to give Rory a diamond ring, then he wanted it to be the best diamond ring there could ever be.

Rory checked her watch. Where was Caleb? They were meant to be going home together, and she preferred Caleb to drive, as she was really struggling to fit behind the steering wheel. And they had an early ante-natal class to attend. She didn't need to for the information, but more for the fact that she wanted to develop friendships with the other mothers in the group, so that she'd have a group of friends she could call on when Caleb went back to work. She was the only one she knew who was scheduled to deliver early, and she'd been lucky to find a group that had begun accepting mothers from twenty-five weeks' pregnant with multiples.

Her phone buzzed in her pocket and she pulled it free. Caleb.

'Hey.'

'Rory? Sorry, I've been pulled into a consult for a lady with pre-eclampsia.'

'Oh. So how late do you think you'll be?'

'Erm…give me half an hour. Is that okay? When's your class?'

Good, he hadn't forgotten. This was important. She was nervous. 'Starts at seven.'

'Okay. I'll get down there as soon as possible. Can you grab a seat in Reception and wait for me? Or go get a drink.'

'Will do.' She ended the call and sighed. Delays in their job were inevitable. Just because the rota said a five p.m. finish, it did not necessarily mean leaving at five pm. Often they could still be in a surgery, or needed to stay late because they want to see a delivery through. Or paperwork could delay them, or a quick consult in A&E. She didn't mind waiting on this occasion. They had plenty of time to get to class and she really didn't want to drive, especially not in rush hour.

So Rory grabbed a drink from a vending machine, sat down in Reception and did a bit of people watching. All manner of lives was found here in a hospital, many individual and unique stories. She gazed at a pregnant woman in a dressing gown, wheeling along her IV pole, and wondered about her story. She'd not met her, so had no idea. And what about the guy pacing up and down outside on his mobile phone, smoking furiously and waving his arms about with his voice raised?

She felt the twins kick and she rubbed at her belly and thought about her daughters. They would be here soon, in just a few more short weeks, and one part of her couldn't wait to see them. The other part was terrified. It was again the lack of control that unnerved her. What if she couldn't do it? What if she couldn't be the mother she hoped she'd be? What if, despite all of his promises, Caleb wasn't there for her and she had to do it all alone? She'd never pictured herself as a single mother. She and Caleb were in a romantic relationship, but they'd made no commitment to one another. It wasn't as if they were married. What if it all went wrong? They would have to split custody. And everybody would know, yet again, that she was a failure. That she had been abandoned.

Rory checked her watch, nervously biting her bottom lip. He should have been here by now! She dialled his number and his phone rang for a moment before being answered by a woman. 'Hello?'

'Who is this?' she asked, worried as to why a woman with a sultry voice had answered Caleb's phone.

'It's Trina, Ms Dotson.'

Trina: one of the midwives who had fawned over Caleb that day, hanging onto his every word as if he were some sort of oracle.

'Where's Caleb?'

'Apologies, he's been called into Theatre on an emergency case.'

'Oh.'

'He said if you were to call that he's sorry, and that he'll try to join you later, but would you mind going to the class on your own?' Trina didn't sound sorry. She sounded fake.

'I'm not meant to be going on my own. He's meant to be there!'

'Sorry.'

Rory ended the call, angry. She knew she shouldn't be. This was part of the job and it wasn't as if he had done so on purpose. It was just having to speak to Trina, rather than Caleb. She knew inwardly that he would be kicking himself for letting her down like this. Or so she hoped. Maybe it was innocent. She had to trust him, or there was no point. But it was so hard!

I guess I'll have go to the ante-natal class on my own, then.

She got up and headed out of the hospital towards the car park. It was quite dark now and, though rush hour traffic would still be filling the roads, she had ample time to get to her class. Squeezing in behind the steering wheel, she adjusted the seat and mirrors and headed off into the traffic. The car was low on petrol, so she stopped off at a garage, filled the tank and treated herself to a pastry to tide her over until after the class, when she could cook herself something proper.

Or maybe Caleb would cook. He liked to and, knowing him, no doubt he would want to for missing out on driving her to class. Maybe they'd snuggle later and she could tell him about her ridiculous reaction to him not being there. Maybe they'd laugh about her hormones playing with her mind.

She arrived at the school hall where the antenatal class was held and waddled in to join the others. Chairs were arranged in a circle, but to one side there was a table for tea, coffee and biscuits, and she got herself a cup of tea and went over to find herself a chair. But she couldn't help but notice that she was the only single one there. Everyone else had brought their partners.

The class was run by a midwife and, after she introduced herself, she went round the circle and asked them each to introduce themselves too. Rory was pleased that every mother there was expecting twins. Most of them were non-identical, but there was one other mother opposite her, Lyla, who was also expecting identical twins, only hers were boys.

The midwife began talking to them about how

to stay active and healthy during their pregnancy. About the importance of good sleep, nutrition and things to avoid, like smoking and alcohol, which Rory was sure they all knew anyway. Even though most of it was information she knew, she sat and listened patiently anyway, because none of these other mothers were doctors or obstetricians, and to them the information was reassuring.

The midwife opened up the floor to questions for a bit and then they were shown simple exercises they could do whilst sitting in a chair and how to treat swollen ankles. Then they were all provided with a beanbag and asked to get down on the floor. They were led through a simple relaxation exercise that Rory actually really enjoyed. So much so, she almost fell asleep, after such a long day on her feet. After that, they were taught simple massages their partners could give to them to help, and how they could look after them to ease any aches and pains as they got into their third trimester.

At the end, they were given time to mingle, and Rory went to talk to Lyla and her husband, Michael. She was a solicitor by trade, her husband was a police officer and their babies were going to be their second and third children.

Rory smiled. 'You're having boys, I think you said?'

'Yes. And you're having two girls.'

She nodded. 'We should see if they want to be friends, when they're old enough to play together.'

Lyla nodded. 'I'd like that. What does your husband do?'

'Oh, we're not married, but we both work at the hospital.'

'Oh! Doing what?'

'We're both obstetric surgeons.'

Lyla laughed. 'Why are you here? I bet you know all of this already!'

Rory laughed with her. She liked Lyla. 'Yeah, but being pregnant with twins…it's different when it's you, and I don't want to miss out on anything. And I thought it would be good to get to know people who are in my position. None of my other friends have had twins. Clearly slacking on that front,' she joked.

Lyla laughed. 'Same. Michael and I don't actually have many friends that have children; they're all building their careers. Well, there's one, but they send theirs to boarding school, so I'm not sure they count. But hey, you should take our number and we should meet up for coffee one day to whine about our aching backs and swollen ankles.'

Rory smiled. 'Sure!' They swapped numbers, and then Rory mingled with a few of the others, but it was hard alone. She kept telling herself it was fine, but she didn't like it. It would have been so much easier for her to mingle with Caleb at her side. He'd said he'd try to make it, but the rest of the class was already starting to depart and he still wasn't here.

She said her goodbyes and headed out to the car park. She shivered in the cold and pulled her coat closer, before squeezing once more behind the steering wheel and starting the engine. The windscreen took a moment to clear and, once she felt warm enough, she eased into the traffic and began the drive home. Twenty minutes and she'd be back home, if she was lucky, cosy in her jammies, sipping tea and getting herself some decent food. She was starving! And hopefully Caleb would get home soon enough to join her and she'd apologise for thinking badly of him.

Pulling out onto the main road, she saw an HGV parked on her side of the road, delivering something to a shop by the looks of it, and she indicated to overtake as the road looked clear.

She was wrong.

Caleb had been called into an emergency caesarean section for his patient, who had developed a placenta praevia—the placenta detaching prematurely from the uterine wall and beginning to bleed. He'd delivered the baby girl, who had needed to be taken to the Special Care Baby

Unit for monitoring, as she'd seemed unable to maintain her oxygen levels. He had thought the emergency part of the surgery was over but then Mum had begun to bleed heavily, haemorrhaging a huge amount. Though they'd tried everything to stop it, they'd had to gain consent from the husband to conduct an emergency hysterectomy, as his patient had been under a general anaesthetic and could not consent herself.

It was a last-ditch attempt to save the mother. Everyone had been on their game, everyone had been focused and Caleb had forgotten everything to make sure that the baby girl he'd delivered had a mother who'd live to take care of her, hold her and love her.

When he made it out of surgery, Caleb glanced at the clock on the wall and realised he'd missed everything meeting Rory, going to class with her and getting home to cook for her.

Damn! I swore I'd never let her down!

Was it impossible never to let her down? The job they did dictated that they wouldn't always get away on time. *Like Dad's did.*

He didn't like comparing himself to his father. It felt extremely uncomfortable. But he comforted himself with the fact that this was just the once, and it was *just* an ante-natal class he'd missed. It wasn't as if he'd missed the birth or anything! It wasn't as if he had missed their first word or their first steps. Rory wouldn't be mad, though she might be slightly upset that for her first time she'd had to go alone. He hoped she'd had a good time.

As he sat there writing his surgical report, he tried to call her on her mobile to apologise, as he wanted to stay at the hospital a bit longer. It was imperative to him that he be there when his patient awoke to explain why she was now infertile and would not be able to carry any more children. He couldn't leave that to someone else. He had made the cuts. He had removed her womb.

Rory didn't answer his call. It rang and rang, but she didn't pick up. Was she mad? Trina had told him that Rory had sounded upset when she'd spoken to her and he knew he'd let her down. He didn't like that he'd made her feel the way his own mother had felt—abandoned, alone. Pushed to one side to make room for her husband's work and patients.

But this was the job! Had he been too quick to judge his father?

And would Rory ever forgive him?

Rory felt as if she was coming out of a deep sleep. She could hear something ringing. A phone…? Bells…? Something sticky was gluing her eyes shut and, as she reached up to clear them, a sharp pain inflamed her shoulder, sickening in its intensity, and its clarifying note brought her back to her reality.

She could hear traffic. Concerned voices. Shouting. Sirens. There was the smell of metal, blood and hot engines. She could feel pain all over her body, and now she was gasping and, despite being unable to open her eyes, realised that *she was upside down* and what felt like a vice was holding her in place.

And then it all came back to her.

She'd been driving, overtaking. Why had she been overtaking? She couldn't think why, but then suddenly there'd been bright-white head-lamps glaring at her, a vehicle zooming towards her! The blare of a horn…her horn?…and then a sickening crunch, an impact. She'd spun, felt her head crack against the side window, as her car had flipped and the world had gone black.

I've been in an accident! I'm hurt! I can't get out!

Her seatbelt held her in place and somewhere in the car she could hear her mobile phone ringing. It was Caleb—that was his ringtone. The one she'd assigned to him, to no-one else. *Where is it? Can I reach it?*

But she couldn't see. The sticky stuff holding her eyes closed was blood. Her head hurt. Her shoulder, her hips, felt like white fire…

My babies!

She cried as she tried to stretch out blindly with her uninjured arm to try and reach the phone, aiming in the general direction of the ringing, but she couldn't get hold of it. Her fingertips found its edge, but she couldn't stretch enough actually to find purchase. Rory screamed out in frustration.

And then it stopped ringing. She felt her heart break in despair. Hot tears coursed over her forehead, instead of her cheeks, and then suddenly she heard a voice. A calm, woman's voice.

'Hey there. Hang on in there, we're going to get you out safely, okay?'

'My babies! I'm pregnant!'

'Okay, okay, what's your name?'

'Rory.'

'Okay, Rory, my name's Chantal and I'm a paramedic. You've been in a car accident and you're currently upside down. We can't get your doors open, as they've been crushed by the impact, but we're going to get you cut out, okay? It's going to take some time. Were you alone in your vehicle?'

'Y-yes! I'm alone. Please! Call Caleb!'

'We will, but first we're going to get you out, okay?'

She tried to nod, but her neck hurt. Everything hurt. It felt as if her blood was pounding in her head, but she knew it just felt that way because she was upside down and her blood was pooling through gravity, making it feel worse than it actually was.

As the fire crew arrived to start stabilising her vehicle so they could cut her free, she tried to remain as calm as she could. Tried to test each of her body parts for movement to see what hurt and what didn't. She could wriggle her toes and move her ankles, which was good. Her legs didn't feel too bad, though she couldn't move them much. Hopefully just cuts and bruises. But her pelvis felt on fire and her chest hurt, as did her shoulder, her arm.

Please just let me and the babies get through this!

'Rory?' Chantal was back at the window. 'We're going to try and get you out now. We've given you something for the pain, but this still might hurt a little, okay?'

'Okay.' She tried to calm her breathing through the oxygen mask that was suddenly placed over her face. Tried not to think too hard about how this was going to feel. Tried not to think too hard about what they might discover when she made it to the hospital…

'Caleb!'

He heard a voice shout behind him just as he was pushing through the security door on Maternity to go home.

He turned and saw Trina running towards him, her face flushed and urgent.

'What is it?'

'We've just had a call come in from Accident and Emergency. Jennifer Boulter.'

The mother with twins with aggressive breast cancer. 'Is she alright?'

Trina shook her head. 'She's bleeding. Pretty heavily, by all accounts, and they've just rung up to ask if there's an obstetric surgeon that can take her into Theatre. Rory's not here and, though Mr Michaels is, with his arm in a cast he can't do surgery. Could you do it?'

Caleb nodded. Of course he would, if there was no-one else. And, though he was tired and exhausted from a super-long day and wanted to get home to Rory, he knew that once he got into Theatre all his own unimportant aches, pains and tiredness would go away.

'Would you call Rory for me at home? Let her know I've been called back into Theatre?'

'Of course.'

'And apologise for me. Tell her the situation— let her know, it couldn't be helped. Thanks.'

He turned and headed back into the unit, full of determination, full of guilt that yet again he was being pulled away from the woman he loved to attend a patient. 'And can someone get the admitting doctor to give me a call so I can get Jennifer's admission details?'

'He's on hold right now, waiting for you.'

Caleb smiled. 'You knew I wouldn't let you down, huh?'

Trina laughed. 'You never do!'

No. He did his best to not let anyone down. He just hoped that Rory wouldn't be too mad that he'd missed the ante-natal class and would now miss having an evening meal with her. He would make it up to her. Maybe he'd take her out for a meal tomorrow night instead—one last night out before the babies came in a couple of weeks. Though he felt guilty about letting her down, it was one ante-natal class. He would go to all the others, hold her hand and do breathing exercises with her, even though she was going to have a caesarean. He would be the best partner. He would be the best dad. He wouldn't be like his own.

There was no way he was going to miss anything important.

Rory slipped in and out of consciousness. She experienced snippets. She could remember being strapped onto a back board, the discomfort of the neck collar and the sharp pinch of needles going into her arms. Could feel something tight and compressing going around her pelvis, causing her to black out. Voices…. Chantal's voice… softly encouraging. The glare of blue lights as she was wheeled along. The slam of the ambulance door closing. The rocking as the vehicle drove. The loud blare of sirens. Something tightening around her upper arm. The hiss of oxygen.

She wanted to say something, remind Chantal to call Caleb, but she was beginning to feel fuzzy and it was becoming hard to focus, to form words, to say how she felt.

'She's crashing!'

Who is crashing? she thought. Not her. Not Chantal…though the paramedic sounded concerned. Something…something was being administered into her arm, something cold pressing against her right chest and lower left abdomen. The lights dimmed. Sound faded.

She felt tired. So tired! And the darkness seemed soft and welcoming, reaching out for her, welcoming her in… And she knew that in the darkness there would be no pain and no fear, and it wanted her to go there, to keep her safe…

So Rory let go.

CHAPTER TWELVE

'I CAN'T STOP this bleeding!' Caleb said, frustration washing over him. He'd delivered Jennifer Boulter's twin boys, both small, Baby A weighing just one pound and three ounces and Baby B weighing a little more, at one pound five ounces. He'd removed them from Jennifer's womb with great care and delicacy as they'd seemed so small, like baby birds, fragile and bony. The NICU team had worked their magic, getting the boys hooked up to ventilators and placed in the warmers, and whisked them back to their department for monitoring and further care.

Caleb was still in Theatre, trying his damnedest to stop her bleeding, trying his best not to have to give another woman an emergency hysterectomy tonight. He knew that sometimes it was necessary. Knew that sometimes it was unavoidable. But he'd already sat at one woman's bedside tonight, waiting for her to wake so that he could deliver the news. He had already sat and answered her questions as she'd cried and mourned a future she'd not yet been ready to lose.

The theatre phone rang and a nurse answered it, as he finally located the source of the bleed. 'What is it?'

The nurse turned to look at him. 'They wanted to let us know that there's an emergency coming up.'

'Another one? I'm not done here!' He didn't like to lose his temper, but with being two surgeons down he was really beginning to feel the load. Rory would be at home, thinking he had abandoned her, and he didn't like that feeling. Nor did he want to have to ask her to come in. She needed her rest.

'It's not for this theatre, it's for Theatre Two.'

'Then why are we being called? Who's operating?' He frowned. 'Have they called Rory in? She's meant to be resting.'

It seemed as if the nurse seemed could hardly look him in the eye. 'They've called in Mr Atwood-Green.'

Caleb frowned. He'd thought James had left for an important dinner with his wife. They were celebrating their anniversary and he had left strict instruction not to be disturbed. They *could* have called Rory, so why hadn't they? Why had they called in the consultant? 'What's the emergency?'

'Pregnant woman in an RTA,' said the nurse quietly.

'Does James want me to tag in after I'm done here?' he asked.

The nurse shook her head. 'No. He said to take your time here.'

'Fine.' At least it meant that he didn't have to worry about the other woman whilst he was taking care of Jennifer. He would absolutely get this poor woman through her surgery so that she could see her babies and have enough strength left over to fight her battle with cancer. The other patient was the other surgeon's worry.

When Caleb had finished and the nurses had begun to wheel Jennifer out of Theatre, the nurse who'd answered the phone came up to him and said, 'There's a doctor waiting for you outside.'

'Who?'

'A Dr Fraser, from A&E.'

'If he needs a consult, he could have just called up on the phone.'

'He needs to speak with you—urgently. It's about…the patient, in Theatre Two.'

James's patient… He frowned at the nurse. Something was going on that he wasn't privy to. He dried his hands and left the scrub room, to find a guy in green scrubs stood waiting for him.

'Mr Stride?'

'Yes?'

'I'd like a word, if I may? Is there somewhere we can sit down?'

Caleb recognised the tone in an instant. It was the tone used with a family member, when there was difficult news to impart. 'Who's hurt?'

'Ms Dotson.'

It took a moment for his brain to process the words, as if the world had slowed down exponentially. He noticed the blue flecks in the man's greyish eyes, noted the tiny scar by his mouth and a thin gold chain around his neck, and then suddenly the world sped up again and his brain made giant leaps. Rory was hurt. She had to be the other woman in Theatre Two with James Atwood-Green! The nurse in Theatre had known and not told him!

The doctor saw the truth dawn in his eyes. 'We couldn't tell you, not whilst you were operating. We needed you to concentrate on your patient. It was Mr Atwood-Green's strict instructions that you not be told who was being brought in.'

He could feel his legs turning to jelly and a wave of nausea washing over him. A hot flush of heat and pounding in his ears made him think that he might pass out.

Rory had been hurt in an RTA. How badly? And the babies? Were the babies alright?

He felt himself be guided over to a seat and felt Dr Fraser's hand on his shoulder.

'What happened?'

'Her car was hit by another car when she went to overtake. I believe her vehicle flipped and rolled and Ms Dotson was trapped inside and had to be cut out.'

'What are her injuries?'

'A fractured pelvis. Dislocated shoulder. She was bleeding heavily and the paramedics got her here as quickly as they…'

Caleb didn't listen to the rest. He had to be with her. He had to know what was going on. He had to be by her side! But before he could get anywhere he felt a hand upon his arm, slowing him down and pulling him back, and suddenly Dr Fraser was blocking him.

'Get out of my way!'

'You can't go in there.'

'That is the love of my life on that table. My daughters!'

'I understand,' said Dr Fraser. 'But Mr Atwood-Green knows what he is doing, and he does not need his focus distracted by having Ms Dotson's partner in Theatre looking over his shoulder and questioning his medical choices. I know you want to be in there, but you can't help her now.'

Caleb wanted to punch him. Wanted to push

him to one side and slam him into a wall, just so that he could get into Theatre.

But…he wasn't a violent man and Dr Fraser was right. He would be nothing but a distraction for James and he did not want to have his attention waver from Rory. She needed him more than she needed Caleb right now.

Caleb sank to his knees and felt tears well up in his eyes. He had failed her. He had failed his babies—he should have been with them! And now he could do nothing to save them.

He would never forgive himself for this.

He couldn't sit still. He needed to pace. He went back and forth, back and forth in the small family room, and when pacing didn't make him feel better he sat again. For a second. And then he realised that sitting made him feel worse and so he got up to pace again.

He'd called everyone that mattered: Rory's mum and her sister, Maylee. They were on their way. He'd called his own mum. She'd called his dad who, not surprisingly, said he'd try to make it, but Caleb knew in his heart that he wouldn't see the man, even though these were his grandchildren. He hadn't been able to turn up for his own children, so why would he turn up for anyone else's?

To think that lately he'd been trying to understand the man and give him some grace for the disappointments of his childhood and life. Thinking that maybe his dad had been in situations like Caleb had today—no-one else available to do a surgery. Or with an emergency that had come in at the last moment.

But every single time, every single time Caleb needed him, there had been an emergency and Callum Stride's patients had taken precedent over his own son. Surely it wasn't possible? Sometimes, maybe, but *every* time? How had the man felt the way Caleb felt now and stayed away? If he'd felt anything at all.

He'd tried to not be like his father, but hadn't he let Rory and his babies down? If he'd been with them, then maybe there might not have been an accident. Maybe they would all be home right now, tucked up in bed, warm, comfortable and fast asleep. Maybe they wouldn't be fighting for their lives if he'd put her first and been with her.

But what could he have done? He'd been needed. There'd been emergencies and no-one else to do them. He'd thought that *this once*, this *one time,* would be okay and that Rory would understand him letting her down. But maybe now she never would. Maybe she would always hate him for not being there. How frightened she must have been in that car—trapped, upside down, hurt, scared for their babies. And *he hadn't been there!*

The door opened and he turned in an instant, hoping it was a nurse with an update, or even better James Atwood-Green come to tell him that everything was alright. That Rory was in recovery and their babies were in the NICU. But it wasn't. It was Rory's mum, eyes red and tearful. She ran into his arms and he hugged her, feeling guilty.

How many people were affected by tonight? Too many.

How would he ever make this good again if one of them was permanently hurt from this? Or, worse, if someone died? How would he ever forgive himself?

How would *they*?

The door opened again and Caleb looked up, stunned to see his father standing awkwardly in the doorway.

'Dad?'

'Caleb.'

'You…you came?' He was surprised. A little stunned.

Callum Stride nodded, looking uncomfortable. 'Of course I did.'

'You never come.'

At this, Callum looked down and away. 'I've

let you down, I know. Many times. But I'm trying to change that now.'

'Not hard enough.' He turned away from his dad. He didn't have the time, or the need, to have this conversation with him right now.

'You're right.'

Surprised, he turned back to look at his father. *'What?'*

'I said you're right. I didn't try hard enough. It was easier to stay at work, to deal with patients, to throw myself into each and every heart surgery, because to me that was easier than facing whatever was going on. I've been cowardly, and most importantly—I've begun to realise through some counselling that I had after my second marriage ended—that I had a responsibility to be there for others and not just for myself.'

'You're having counselling?'

Callum nodded. 'I tried to be there for you all and for your mother. God knows I tried, but the fear that I felt when you were born too soon was too much. I was overwhelmed by my own feelings, my own fears. And yet somehow I had to deal with your mother's too and it was all too much. It made me feel like I was going to explode, and so I left. It was the only way for me to cope. I know that it was wrong, and I continued to be wrong, but I just thought every time you got hurt or injured or sick would make me feel the same way, so I *avoided* it. It seemed easier, even though I knew that it was upsetting to you that I wasn't there. Upsetting to your mother to make her go through things alone.

'The drama of home and relationships was always too much for me, but when you added moments like appendicitis or broken bones... You have to understand, son, that I wanted to be with you, but didn't know how to deal with how I felt. You were this whirlwind of energy for me, and your mum would be crying. and I couldn't cope with that. I hated how it made me feel. And you wanted to be held all the time and I just couldn't... I've always struggled with strong emotions, so it just seemed easier to stay away. I told myself it was easier for *me,* even though I knew it was hurting *you.* I didn't understand it, but now I do. Like I say, it's no excuse, but I wanted you to know that I'm trying to be better.'

Caleb remembered his mother sitting with Caleb on her knee, comforting him after a fall, and saying she would hold him enough for the both of them. That she wasn't used to being held by his father either.

His father was right. It wasn't an excuse.

Dad loved me, he just couldn't show it.

He felt tears threaten at the realisation that he'd been fighting his father his whole life, when they should have just talked! His father had tried to call him, had left messages, and Caleb had simply ignored them. He'd given his father a taste of his own medicine. Had abandoned him. Maybe he was more like his father than he actually realised.

'Can I hug you?' he asked.

His father nodded, tears glazing his eyes, and he ran into his father's arms and began to sob.

A moment after, just after they were both regaining their composure, the door opened softly. 'Caleb?' It was James.

'Are they alright?'

James nodded. 'They're all going to be just fine.'

CHAPTER THIRTEEN

WHEN RORY CAME TO, she was in a hospital room, the steady beep of an ECG monitor beside her, intravenous lines going into both arms, and she felt exhausted; woozy and exhausted. At first, she couldn't remember why she was there, and then the memory of the car crash came cascading into her brain all at once, and the ECG beeps accelerated as she gazed down and realised her bump was gone. Thirty weeks' pregnant and her bump was gone! Where were her babies?

'Hey.'

She turned to her right and realised that Caleb was there, holding her right hand, smiling with tears falling down his face.

'Caleb? Where are the girls? Are they…?' She almost couldn't bring herself to ask the question. 'Alright?'

He smiled. 'They're good. Strong! They're in the NICU and your mum and my parents are with them.'

'They're okay? You promise? You wouldn't lie to me?' She had to make sure.

'I could never lie to you, but I'm so sorry I wasn't with you, Rory. I should have been! But I got called into an emergency and then another and... I'm making excuses, I know.'

'When can I go see them? I have to see them and know that they're alright.' She knew Caleb felt bad about letting her down, but that was the least of her problems right now. All she wanted was to see her babies.

'Not yet. You fractured your pelvis and dislocated your shoulder. You have two fine rib fractures. They want to make sure you're stable.'

'I have to go to them!' She tried to move, to rise and get out of bed, but piercing and intense white-hot pain penetrated the fog of her body and she collapsed back down against the pillows in tears.

'Don't move, Rory.'

'How am I supposed to care for them if I can't move? It's my job to protect them!'

'It's *our* job, and I will make sure they're okay until we're able to get you up there to look at them.'

She looked at him, her eyes filling with hot tears. 'I was so scared and you weren't there!'

He looked down and nodded. 'I know, and I'm so sorry.'

'I felt so alone in that car. In pain, frightened.'

He looked full of guilt, burdened by the weight of all that had happened. 'I'm so sorry.'

'It wasn't your fault,' she whispered.

Caleb looked up at her, surprised. 'You don't blame me?'

'I *did* in the moment, when I was scared and panicked and not thinking straight. I thought if you'd been with me, then the accident would never have happened and I wouldn't have gone alone. But…we're surgeons. And we don't have a normal nine-to-five job.' She frowned then, as a thought came to her. 'Who delivered me?'

'James did.'

'He wasn't at the hospital.'

'We called him in.'

'He can't have been happy about that.'

'I think his wife might have been annoyed. It was their anniversary dinner—twenty-five years. But… I think she understands.'

Rory drifted for a while then. Her eyes grew heavy and she let herself drift into the murky world of dreams. When she came to later, it was dark outside and Caleb still sat beside her, fast asleep, his head resting on her bed.

She smiled at him. At his handsome face. At his dedication to her. Yes, she had cursed him for not being there when she'd had her accident, but it had not been his fault. He had stayed at the hospital to save lives. To make sure another couple had got their family safely. Would she have respected him if he'd walked away from that to be with her at an ante-natal class? No. Because that wasn't who they were.

But for how long would he stay at her bedside? What would happen when he realised that twins were hard work and that they were going to have difficult days? Arguments, perhaps, disagreements over how to raise the girls. He could still so easily walk away from them all and her heart broke at the thought of it.

Whilst she'd been pregnant, and especially in these last few weeks, she'd allowed herself to dream of them having a happy-ever-after. But since this accident, and the fact that life gave no certainties or assurances, perhaps she was being naïve in believing happy-ever-afters existed at all. Maybe it did for James and his wife—twenty-five years and still going strong! But it was never the thing to happen to her. Her life had already been filled with disasters: a non-existent father who'd walked out on her as a baby. A fiancé who had walked out on her and left her standing in the church alone. A car crash that had tried to take her life and that of her children. Was it luck that she was still here? Or just the world seeing how many punishments she could take for believing that she could be happy?

Caleb stirred and rubbed his eyes, before lifting his head and realising that she was awake. 'Hey.'

'Hey.'

'You should go home. Get some decent sleep, if you're exhausted.'

'I'm fine right here.'

'Seriously, Caleb. You don't have to stick around for my disaster of a life. Clearly I'm a bad luck charm and I've already traumatised your life enough. I'm giving you an out before life gets really tough.' She tried to smile and be brave about it. But she would deal with it, if he decided to walk away, because she was used to dealing with life's curveballs all on her own. Better to be in charge of being left behind than just let it happen.

'What are you going on about?'

'It's going to be hard, looking after baby twins, whilst also caring for their mother with a broken pelvis, and working! It's going to be impossible, and it's okay. I'll do it. Mum will rally round, and Maylee, and…we'll deal with it.'

'I don't care that it's going to be hard. And I could never walk away from my children, or you, so stop saying things like this!'

She sighed. 'You never wanted this.'

'Neither did you! But things change. Life changes. People change!' He stared at her. 'Are you telling me that you don't want me?'

She shook her head. 'No. I do. I want you very

much, but I know from experience that the people I want to stick around very rarely do, so…'

'I love you, Rory, and I will not let you push me away.'

She stared at him, shocked by his words. He loved her? He'd never said that before!

'Leo might have been a fool, but *I'm* not! You are the single most amazing person in my entire life. Ever since you walked into it, I have not been able to get you out of my mind and my heart, and I couldn't tear you out of them if I tried. *Which I will not!* I love you and I love our girls and I will be here for all of you, for all of our life together. In fact…'

He rummaged in his pocket and then pulled forth a small box. 'I was going to save this until later, but I'm going to do it now.' He flipped the lid and presented her with a solitaire diamond ring. 'Rory Dotson…will you marry me?'

Mouth open, Rory gazed, shocked and stupefied, between the ring and him and then back again. He wanted to marry her? 'Are you sure?'

'Surer than I have ever been in my life! You are my world, and I will dedicate every single day of our lives together to proving to you that you are the very air that I breathe. That I will love you and care for you, no matter what. That I will make you and our girls a priority—subject to work emergencies, of course.'

He smiled, knowing and accepting that of course they were unavoidable. That his father had not deserted him, had not considered his sisters, his mother and him as second best, or somehow less important. That he'd simply been struggling with something that was at the core of who he was. That he hadn't been able to change it.

Rory sobbed a laugh. Shock, surprise, awe and delight all washed over her in a happy wave, and she cried, 'Yes!' as he slipped the ring onto her finger.

Caleb stood and leaned over the bed, kissing her. It felt so good to feel his lips pressed against hers. To feel his love for her embrace her, envelop her, and she felt a fool for not realising the depth of his love before. She'd just been so used to not being good enough that she'd just assumed that Caleb would eventually run from her when things got tough. The way Leo had. She'd seen countless fathers not turn up for the birth of their children, abandoning their partners right at the crucial moment, as realisation hit of what their lives were about to be.

She'd simply accepted the same. She'd forgotten that Caleb was nothing like anyone else. He'd always been different. Always special. And she'd been so afraid to allow herself to love him, in case he ripped her heart out.

Well, not any more.

'I've spoken to the doctors. We're going to wheel you up to NICU in your bed. You can look at the babies through the viewing window.'

'Can I touch them? Hold them?'

He smiled. 'One step at a time, my love.'

In her mind, it took far too long to happen, but hours later, when James was happy that she was stable, he allowed her to be transported up to the NICU. She felt nervous. Excited. Apprehensive. Caleb had told her that the babies were good weights for their gestation, and the fact that there'd been the beginning of TTTS. Twin A, the bigger twin, had weighed three pounds, four ounces, and Twin B just under three pounds. Not huge, but bigger than some babies she'd seen in the NICU.

Then she was there. Her girls' incubators had been moved next to the viewing window and she could see them, wearing little knitted bonnets, one pink, one yellow. They looked so vulnerable and small, covered in wires and monitoring equipment, but they were stable and unhurt by the accident. Her body had taken most of the impact, cushioning them, protecting them—even if, as Caleb had told her, the placenta had been torn and begun bleeding profusely at the scene.

She used to come to this window when life got too much. But now she had been brought here to see her own babies inside and she realised just how strong she actually was. She would heal and her babies would grow.

Rory pressed her hand to the window, straining to see them. She wanted to touch them. 'They should have names. They need their names,' she said, when she saw their cards saying just Twin A Dotson and Twin B Dotson.

'What were you thinking?'

They'd kept lists individually on their phones. They'd occasionally discussed it, but had agreed that they'd need to see them first to see what names suited. 'She looks like a Zoe,' she said, gazing at her bigger daughter. 'It means life, doesn't it?'

Caleb smiled. 'Zoe… I like it. What about our other girl?'

'You should name her. It's only fair we get one each!'

'Okay. What about Brianna? It means strong.'

'Zoe and Brianna.' Rory smiled, tears of happiness falling down her cheeks. 'I want to hold them. Can I hold them?'

Caleb smiled. 'I'll fetch the nurse.'

It took some doing—a lot of arranging of cables and fetching extra blankets to keep the girls warm when they were removed from their incubators—but eventually they were placed into Rory's arms.

With Caleb sitting beside her, supporting the

arm on the side she'd dislocated, she'd never felt such happiness! Her world was complete. She didn't need anything more.

She had Caleb, Zoe and Brianna.

Her bones and body would heal. Her girls would grow stronger.

And she knew that, with them all by her side, and her heart filled with love, it could never be broken.

EPILOGUE

RORY WAS NERVOUS as she stood outside the church in her wedding dress, holding her bouquet of freesias, roses and baby's breath. There was no doubt in her mind about Caleb. She already knew he was inside, waiting for her. It was just the thought of standing in front of everyone she knew, having to speak. She'd never had a problem talking to patients, because that was only ever one or two people—sometimes three or four, if family had arrived at the hospital to coo over the new baby in the family. But speaking in front of a full church in front of friends, family and co-workers… She loved them all, but it was still a daunting thing.

And she wanted her voice to ring true, sure and confident as she said her vows, because she wanted Caleb to know that his love for her had made her that way. He'd given her strength that she'd never known she had. The strength to face another wedding day. The strength to be a mother. A wife.

The last year and a half, since the girls had

been born, had been difficult only with regard to her recovery from the accident. Her fractured pelvis had caused her an awful lot of pain and she'd not been able to care for Zoe and Briana the way she'd wanted to. But Caleb had been there for them all, lifting the girls and putting them on her lap for story time or cuddles; helping her bathe them and putting them to bed. He'd done a lot of the heavy lifting!

They stood before her now with one of the bridesmaids. Zoe and Brianna were flower girls and they'd practised spreading the rose petals in the weeks prior. Right now they were eager to start throwing the petals about.

'Not yet, girls. You have to wait until you hear the music. You have to wait until you go inside the church and see Daddy.'

Zoe and Brianna adored their father and he adored them. She could hardly believe the fact that Caleb had once told her that he'd never wanted to be a father. He was the best! He'd even healed his relationship with his own father, which had been amazing to see, and Rory had been glad to get to know Callum Stride. He was a talented and dedicated doctor. Yes, he did struggle with social obligations, but he was trying new things. Challenging himself to do things that previously he had avoided or found uncomfortable.

Zoe and Brianna had brought their family

neatly together, as if they were the threads that had pulled two halves back into one.

The music began and her nerves became all aflutter.

'Are you ready?' her mum asked.

'I am.'

There was a little last-minute fiddling with the veil, and her bridesmaids arranged the back of her dress and straightened her train so that it would be seen in its full glory as she walked down the aisle.

Then the doors opened and her stomach flipped as she saw everyone inside turning to look. And then her chief bridesmaid began to lead Zoe and Brianna down the aisle. They looked beautiful, like two flower fairies in their pure white dresses and floral headbands that matched Rory's bouquet, tossing rose petals up into the air and all around, making everyone in the church smile and giggle.

Then Rory began to walk forward, escorted by her mother. Her eyes met Caleb's and suddenly all her nerves and all her worries went away.

This was a day of celebration.

A day of love and unification.

She could do anything she wanted in this world, knowing how much she loved him and how much he loved her.

And they would raise their girls to be strong, confident women, adored by both parents who wanted nothing more than for them to be happy and healthy.

'You look beautiful,' Caleb said as she came to stand by her side.

Rory smiled, her heart filled with her love for him, and passed her bouquet back to her chief bridesmaid. Zoe and Brianna were still throwing out petals, which made her smile.

She turned and faced her husband-to-be and took his hands in hers.

Ready to say their vows.

Ready to commit to the rest of their lives together.

This had to be what bliss felt like.

* * * * *

If you enjoyed this story, check out
these other great reads from
Louisa Heaton

The Surgeon's Relationship Ruse
Finding a Family Next Door
Best Friend to Husband?
Resisting the Single Dad Surgeon

All available now!

Get up to 4 Free Books!

We'll send you 2 free books from each series you try PLUS a free Mystery Gift

FORGOTTEN GREEK PROPOSAL

HIS ROYAL BRIDE REPLACEMENT

FREE Value Over **$25**

Finding a Family Next Door

A Kiss Under the Northern Lights

Both the **Harlequin Presents** and **Harlequin Medical Romance** series feature exciting stories of passion and drama.

YES! Please send me 2 FREE novels from Harlequin Presents or Harlequin Medical Romance and my FREE gift (gift is worth about $10 retail). After receiving them, if I don't wish to receive any more books, I can return the shipping statement marked "cancel." If I don't cancel, I will receive 6 brand-new larger-print novels every month and be billed just $7.19 each in the U.S., or $7.99 each in Canada, or 4 brand-new Harlequin Medical Romance Larger-Print books every month and be billed just $7.19 each in the U.S. or $7.99 each in Canada, a savings of 20% off the cover price. It's quite a bargain! Shipping and handling is just 50¢ per book in the U.S. and $1.25 per book in Canada.* I understand that accepting the 2 free books and gift places me under no obligation to buy anything. I can always return a shipment and cancel at any time. The free books and gift are mine to keep no matter what I decide.

Choose one: ☐ **Harlequin Presents Larger-Print** (176/376 BPA G36Y)   ☐ **Harlequin Medical Romance** (171/371 BPA G36Y)   ☐ **Or Try Both!** (176/376 & 171/371 BPA G36Z)

Name (please print)

Address   Apt. #

City   State/Province   Zip/Postal Code

Email: Please check this box ☐ if you would like to receive newsletters and promotional emails from Harlequin Enterprises ULC and its affiliates. You can unsubscribe anytime.

Mail to the Harlequin Reader Service:
IN U.S.A.: P.O. Box 1341, Buffalo, NY 14240-8531
IN CANADA: P.O. Box 603, Fort Erie, Ontario L2A 5X3

Want to explore our other series or interested in ebooks? Visit www.ReaderService.com or call 1-800-873-8635.

---

*Terms and prices subject to change without notice. Prices do not include sales taxes, which will be charged (if applicable) based on your state or country of residence. Canadian residents will be charged applicable taxes. Offer not valid in Quebec. This offer is limited to one order per household. Books received may not be as shown. Not valid for current subscribers to the Harlequin Presents or Harlequin Medical Romance series. All orders subject to approval. Credit or debit balances in a customer's account(s) may be offset by any other outstanding balance owed by or to the customer. Please allow 4 to 6 weeks for delivery. Offer available while quantities last.

Your Privacy—Your information is being collected by Harlequin Enterprises ULC, operating as Harlequin Reader Service. For a complete summary of the information we collect, how we use this information and to whom it is disclosed, please visit our privacy notice located at https://corporate.harlequin.com/privacy-notice. Notice to California Residents – Under California law, you have specific rights to control and access your data. For more information on these rights and how to exercise them, visit https://corporate.harlequin.com/california-privacy. For additional information for residents of other U.S. states that provide their residents with certain rights with respect to personal data, visit https://corporate.harlequin.com/other-state-residents-privacy-rights/.

HPHM25

—